C O R A L R

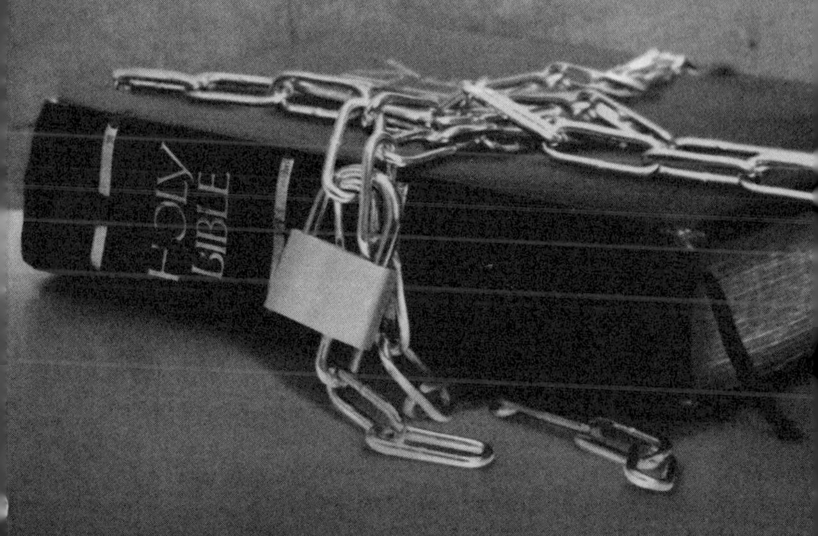

10 TRUTHS about HATE CRIME LAWS

TEN TRUTHS ABOUT HATE CRIME LAWS

by John Aman

Cover and Interior Design: Roark Creative, www.roarkcreative.com

Published by Coral Ridge Ministries

Printed in the United States of America

Post Office Box 1920
Fort Lauderdale, Florida 33302
1-800-988-7884
www.coralridge.org
letters@coralridge.org

CONTENTS

CONTENTS

JOHN AMAN

Coral Ridge Ministries
Fort Lauderdale, Florida

FREE SPEECH

RELIGIOUS

EFFICIENT LAW ENFORCEMENT

LIBERTY

SOCIAL HARMONY

FAMILY

EQUAL JUSTICE

HATE CRIME LAWS INVADE THE SANCTITY OF THE MIND AND GIVE GOVERNMENT AUTHORITY OVER WHAT WE THINK.

INTRODUCTION

"Fairly charged up" after just hearing his pastor discuss homosexuality, David Ott stopped at a Madison, Wisconsin, carwash and tried to talk to a fellow customer about the topic. Ott saw the gay pride sticker on the man's car and, as a former homosexual, he wanted to share how he had found freedom from that lifestyle. However, when Ott said that he had "been down this road before, and you may wish to reconsider where this leads," the other customer became angry.[1]

"Don't lay any of your Bible-thumping BS on me!" Ott recalled the man saying. "If you don't leave me alone, I'm gonna kick your... tail." That ended the matter, or so Ott thought.

Five months later, police arrived at Ott's door to charge him with disorderly conduct. Normally, he would have faced a $500 fine, but since the charge was disorderly conduct toward a homosexual, the hate crime "penalty enhancer" upped the possible sentence to one year in jail and a $10,000 fine.

PENALIZED: Authorities in Madison, Wisconsin, charged David Ott with a hate crime and forced him to attend sensitivity training and do 50 hours of community service. His legal bill was $7,000.

Ott, who has a wife and two sons, settled the case and was ordered to attend sensitivity training, do 50 hours of community service, and was placed on probation for one year. His legal bill was $7,000.[2] Two lesbians taught his sensitivity training seminar, where the primary lesson, Ott said, "was the fact that homosexual behavior is not immoral. That was the number one premise of the conference."

"Nobody once during this entire proceeding ever bothered to ask me if I hated the guy," Ott said later, "which is really interesting, because I wasn't motivated by hatred at all. I was actually motivated by compassion, because I see where these people are ending up in these lifestyles and it's painful for me to see that."[3]

What's Wrong With Hate Crime Laws?

David Ott's ordeal showcases much of what is wrong with hate crime laws. They criminalize speech, violate religious liberty, give special protection to certain groups, mete out vastly disproportionate penalties, and subject "violators" to moral re-education classes.

Widely used, "hate crime" is an ambiguous term that first arose in the 1980s. It refers to the presence of bias or prejudice in crimes against certain designated groups. But prejudice is subjective and no one can say just how much bias must be present to turn a garden-variety crime into a full-blown "hate crime." For its purposes, the federal government defines a hate crime as any "criminal offense ... which is motivated, *in whole or in part*, by the offender's bias against a race, religion, disability, sexual orientation, or ethnicity/national origin." But how and when bias must be evident and just how much bias must be present to constitute a hate crime are all slippery questions that have no concrete answers.

That fact has not hindered the success of the hate crime movement. While the effort to add "hate crime" laws to state legal codes is barely 30 years old, all but five states now criminalize bias-motivated violence and intimidation. Twenty-nine states give special protection to "sexual orientation" in their hate crime laws.[4]

The rapid adoption of hate crime statutes across the country is due in large part to the fact that voting for laws that punish prejudice is something that has no political downside for most legislators. "The hate crime laws provided an opportunity to denounce two evils—crime and bigotry—without offending any constituencies or spending any money," according to James B. Jacobs and Kimberly Potter.[5]

Time to Take a Second Look

But, as hate crime horror stories multiply—(a few are told in this book)—some legislators may be willing to take a second look at hate crime laws. After Pennsylvania's Supreme Court removed "sexual orientation," gender, and physical and mental disability from the state's hate crime statute in July 2008, there was immediate pressure on the legislature to restore those groups to the law's coverage. The chairman of the state Senate Judiciary committee said he would be willing to review the court's ruling, but he made it clear that "all constitutional implications involved, including freedom of speech, must be fully understood."[6]

More legislative bodies nationwide should do the same. James Madison wrote in 1785 that "it is proper to take alarm at the first experiment on our liberties." America's Founders, he wrote, anticipated threats to freedom and took preemptive action.

James Madison
(Library of Congress)

The free men of America did not wait till usurped power had strengthened itself by exercise, and entangled the question in precedents. They saw all the consequences in the principle, and they avoided the consequences by denying the principle.[7]

A Clear and Present Danger

After thirty years, "hate crimes" laws are no longer an experiment. They are, as *Ten Truths About Hate Crime Laws* set out to show, a clear and present danger to free speech, religious liberty, equal justice, social harmony, efficient law enforcement, and the family.

"Hate crime" laws invade the sanctity of the mind and give government authority over what we think—something that is entirely alien to the American tradition of liberty. As the U.S. Supreme Court said in 1943,

> **If there is any fixed star in our constitutional constellation, it is that no official, high or petty, can prescribe what shall be orthodox in politics, nationalism, religion, or other matters of opinion or force citizens to confess by word or act their faith therein."[8]**

This book demonstrates what happens when social engineers rewrite our laws and clarifies why Christians must act now to preserve our precious liberties of freedom of speech and freedom of worship.

TRUTH 1

“Hate Crimes” Are Not Crimes of Hate

It was the perfect "hate crime." Backers of hate crime legislation in Washington—and their allies in the homosexual lobby—could not have hoped for anything better.

Suddenly, here was evidence of America's "hate crime epidemic" blasted to the nation and the world via wall-to-wall media coverage. The need to immediately pass hate crime legislation was evident.

Matthew Shepard, it was reported, had died at the hands of two bigots enraged by his homosexuality. They mercilessly beat him with a .357 magnum pistol, stole $30, and left him tied to a split-rail fence outside Laramie, Wyoming. Alone, in near-freezing nighttime temperatures, the 21-year-old college student fell into a coma and was not found until 18 hours later.[9] He died on October 12, 1998, six days after the brutal attack.[10]

Two days later, crowds gathered in cities nationwide[11] for candlelight vigils in memory of Matthew. Five-thousand people gathered on the steps of the U.S. Capitol to listen to Ellen DeGeneres, Ted Kennedy, and Barney Frank,[12] an openly homosexual member of the U.S. House of Representatives, condemn the murder and call for passage of hate crime legislation.

RALLY: Actress Ellen DeGeneres spoke in memory of Matthew Shepard and called for passage of hate crime legislation during a rally at the Capitol October 14, 1998, in Washington, D.C.

(Randall Links/Associated Press)

"We take issue with those who say that we don't need these laws," House Democratic Leader Richard Gephardt of Missouri told the crowd, as it chanted "Now, Now, Now,"[13] and demanded that Congress pass hate crime legislation before it adjourned. In a written statement, Gephardt also said, "Despite the hurt we all feel, now is not a time for vengeance or anger or finger pointing."[14]

Who Is to Blame?

Few heeded that message. Homosexual rights groups, some in the media, and even a few politicians, charged that Christians who oppose homosexuality were to blame for Matthew Shepard's death. Elizabeth Birch, executive director of the Human Rights Campaign, the nation's largest homosexual advocacy group, charged on NBC's *Today Show* that Shepard was murdered because "people's minds have been twisted with cruel stereotypes about gay and lesbian people."[15] Birch blamed a pro-family ad campaign featuring men and women who had left homosexuality, for having "poisoned" the atmosphere.

BLAMED: Homosexual advocates linked Matthew Shepard's death to pro-family ads featuring people freed from homosexuality by Christ.

The "Truth and Love" print and TV ad campaign, a project of Coral Ridge Ministries and other pro-family groups, had profiled people who found liberation from homosexuality through faith in Jesus Christ. These ads, Birch said, presented homosexuals "as defective, as less than, as not fully human," and she charged that they led to Matthew Shepard's death when he crossed paths with "someone that had been fed this rhetoric and came at him full of rage and hate."

The San Francisco Board of Examiners concurred. A week after Shepard's death, the Board sent a frenzied letter to Coral Ridge Ministries and other pro-family groups denouncing their "hateful rhetoric against gays, lesbians, and transgendered people."[16] There is a "direct correlation," the San Francisco Board wrote, between calling homosexual behavior sinful and the "horrible crimes committed against gays and lesbians," including the death of Matthew Shepard.

Toward hope and healing for homosexuals.

I'm living proof that Truth can set you free.

"Recently, several prominent people like Trent Lott, Reggie White, and Angie and Debbie Winans have spoken out on homosexuality...calling it a sin. When I was living as a lesbian I didn't like hearing words like that...until I realized that God's love was truly meant for me."

One boy's sin and the making of a lesbian.

"I was four years old when a teenage boy molested me. When he warned me not to say a thing, I went silent. But as I grew, the pain wouldn't stay quiet. It would shout when I made male friends. It laughed when I tried to feel pretty. It told me I was unlovable. But saddest of all, when I wanted to turn to my parents to make everything all right – it wouldn't let me tell them why."

Being a woman became a mystery.

"By the time I hit my teens I was tough...my heart cold. I believed being *'feminine'* meant being weak and vulnerable...so looking and dressing hard felt right. I had so thoroughly rejected my own femininity that, even though I had a lot of male friends, I just wasn't attracted to men sexually. I became drawn to other women who had what I felt was missing in me. But the pain inside kept yelling."

There's a God-shaped hole in everyone's heart.

"My sexual attraction to women blossomed in college, and after a gay counselor affirmed my feelings I joined the campus gay/lesbian group. But it was in the course of those group meetings that I knew something was still missing. While I longed for a female life-partner, I knew it just wouldn't work. That's when I went home and prayed, *'God, please show me who You are, and fill the void in my heart.'*"

Knock and He'll answer. But the next step is still yours.

"Change didn't come overnight. Within six months I'd made a firm decision to forsake homosexuality, but I still had sexual desire for women. Even though I filled my days with Christian activity, I fell back into a relationship with someone who quickly became my priority in life, over work, over family and friends...over God. By now the pain inside was throbbing, and my delight eroded into conviction, deception and emotional instability."

Thousands of ex-gays like those here walked away from their homosexual identities. While the paths each took into homosexuality may vary, their stories of hope and healing through the transforming love of Jesus Christ are the same.

Ex-gay ministries throughout the U.S. work daily with homosexuals seeking change, and many provide outreach programs to their families and loved ones.

Once God answers He never hangs up.

"I knew I was running from God, and one day just put it to him: *'Lord, You know that I really enjoy this lifestyle, but I want You to be my first love. I need Your help. I need You to change my heart.'* Shortly after that prayer, I met a Christian woman, *a former lesbian*, who listened patiently to my story and led me to a ministry helping people overcome homosexuality. Because they loved me without judgement, I was able to finally give all my relationships to God, and begin the real road to healing."

Changing hearts. Changing lives.

"Leaving homosexuality was the hardest thing I've ever had to do. I finally saw the patterns of my same-sex attraction and came to understand the underlying needs that had sparked my longings. As I grew in my relationship with God, I knew He had changed me forever. Gone was the hardness. Gone was the hurt. And gone was the shrill cry inside, replaced with God's still, small voice. In His gentle love I found forgiveness, and the acceptance I sought so hard on my own."

There is another way out.

Please, if you, or someone you know or love, is struggling with homosexuality, show them this story. If you truly love someone, you'll tell them the truth. *And the truth that God loves them could just be the truth that sets them free.*

If you really love someone, you'll tell them the truth.

For information on contacting an ex-gay ministry in your area or contacting Parents and Friends of Ex-gays, please call 800-264-6877

In the public interest, this message is sponsored by the following organizations, representing millions of American families:

Alliance for Traditional Marriage - Hawaii
American Family Association
Americans for Truth About Homosexuality
Center for Reclaiming America
Christian Family Network
Christian Coalition
Citizens for Community Values
Colorado For Family Values
Concerned Women for America
Coral Ridge Ministries
Exodus International
Family First
Family Research Council
Kerusso Ministries
Liberty Counsel
Mission America
National Legal Foundation
Straight From The Heart

The True Story

Matthew Shepard's death made him an immediate cause célèbre for homosexual rights. The grim saga of this young man's horrible murder, coupled with the claim that he was targeted because of his homosexuality, has reached millions through documentaries, stage productions, and made-for-TV movies.

Ten years after his death, Matthew Shepard's name is now synonymous with the campaign to enact hate crime laws. Supporters of the "Matthew Shepard Local Law Enforcement Hate Crimes Prevention Act of 2007," are seeking to add "sexual orientation" to the list of groups granted special protection against hate crimes.

There is just one problem with this story. According to the evidence, *it is not true.* Money for drugs, not "homophobia," was the motive for Matthew Shepard's murder, as revealed by a 2004 ABC News *20/20* report.[17] Aaron McKinney, sentenced in 1999 to two life sentences for Matthew Shepard's murder, was on a sleepless week-long methamphetamine binge and in search of money for more drugs when he and his accomplice, Russell Henderson, met Shepard at a bar.

Earlier that evening, McKinney said, he had tried and failed to take $10,000 from a drug dealer. He saw in Shepard, a

"I would say it wasn't a hate crime,

all I wanted to do was beat him up and rob him."

—Aaron McKinney

well-dressed but slight young man, an easy robbery victim and readily obliged when Shepard asked for a lift home because he was too drunk. All three were in the front seat of McKinney's truck, with Henderson driving, when Shepard grabbed McKinney's leg. McKinney reacted by hitting Shepard with his gun but, as he told ABC, "I was getting ready to pull it on him anyway."

"It Wasn't a Hate Crime"

McKinney's attorney offered a "gay panic" defense at trial, suggesting that the murderer turned violent when Shepard made a homosexual pass at him. McKinney, who will never be eligible for parole, now says that was not the case. "No, I did not," he replied when asked if he attacked Shepard because he was homosexual. "I would say it wasn't a hate crime," he told ABC. "All I wanted to do was beat him up and rob him."

Henderson also denied the hate crime charge. "It's not because me and Aaron had anything against gays or anything like that," he said.[18]

McKinney's girlfriend Kristen Price agrees. Price supported the "gay panic defense" during the trial, but told ABC, "I don't think it was a hate crime at all. I never did."

Cal Rerucha, the prosecutor, said, "I don't think the proof was there," for the hate crime allegation.[19] Rerucha, who sought the death penalty for McKinney, thinks it was McKinney's drug-addled state that led to the crime. "The methamphetamine just fueled to this point where there was no control. It was a horrible, horrible, horrible murder. It was a murder that was once again driven by drugs," he said.[20]

Laramie Police Detective Ben Fritzen, a lead investigator in the case, said, "Matthew Shepard's sexual preference or sexual orientation certainly wasn't the motive in the homicide. If it wasn't Shepard, they would have found another easy target. What it came down to really is drugs and money and two punks that were out looking for it."[21]

"Don't Confuse Me With the Facts"

But these after-trial claims have had little impact on public perceptions. Judy and Dennis Shepard reject the ABC report, as do homosexual advocacy groups. A decade after his death, the story line that Matthew Shepard's killers acted out of hatred for homosexuals remains firmly in place. *Detroit Free Press* columnist Rochelle Riley wrote in 2008 that Shepard "would have been 31 this year had the antigay terrorists not gotten him."[22]

In one sense, it really doesn't matter whether Matthew's murder was a robbery gone bad or the act of two bigots. Either way, justice was done in the end. Wyoming has no hate crime law, but both men are locked up for life. Ironically, McKinney might have faced the death penalty had not Judy Shepard intervened against it.[23]

In the end, the Matthew Shepard story stands to show that when it comes to meting out justice, laws against "hate crimes" are an unneeded solution. In fact, they're a solution in search of a problem.

TRUTH 2

Hate Crime Laws Are a Solution in Search of a Problem

It's bad. It will only get worse. That, in brief, is the overblown assessment from many in academia, the media, and politics on the threat posed to our nation by what authors Jack Levin and Jack McDevitt have called "the rising tide of bigotry and bloodshed."

Levin and McDevitt, both professors at Northeastern University, announced in 1993,

> **It has become nearly impossible to keep track of the shocking rise in brutal attacks directed against individuals because they are black, Latino, Asian, white, disabled, women, or gay .... As ugly as this situation is now, it is likely to worsen throughout the remainder of the decade and into the next century as the forces of bigotry continue to gain momentum.[24]**

"Hate crimes," according to a 1997 U.S. Justice Department policy training manual, are "one of the Nation's most insidious problems."[25]

Ten years later, that "insidious" problem had become, in the words of U.S. Sen. Benjamin L. Cardin, "an epidemic of hate crimes and intimidation occurring nationwide from Jena, Louisiana, to College Park, Maryland."[26]

New York Times readers learned in 2007 that "the level of hate crimes in the United States is astoundingly high—more than 190,000 incidents per year, according to a 2005 Department of Justice study."[27]

What Are the True Numbers?

The FBI reports a much different picture. The number of so-called hate crimes reported to the FBI dropped eight percent between 1995 and 2006. There were 9,895 "bias motivation" offenses reported in 1995.[28] Eleven years later, there were 9,080.[29]

The fabulous claim in the *New York Times* that 190,000 "hate crime" incidents take place annually—a number 21 times greater than what the FBI reported for 2006—stems from a national survey which employed a much looser definition for "hate" than that employed by the FBI. It also illustrates just how ambiguous and subjective the entire "hate crime" enterprise is. "Hate" is very much in the eye of the beholder.

The National Crime Victimization Survey, which yielded the chart-topping numbers for hate crimes reported in the *New York Times*, relied on victims' own reports. In addition, it used a definition for "hate" that cast the net just about as widely as possible. It counted as a hate crime any offense in which, at a minimum, the offender was said to have used "derogatory language."[30] As the 2005 Justice Department review of the survey put it, with some understatement, "This may or may not be an accurate way to evaluate whether the crime was a hate crime."[31]

OVERBLOWN: Despite claims that America faces a "rising tide of bigotry and bloodshed," FBI statistics show a decline from 1995 to 2006.

A Closer Look at the Numbers

Not only has the number of "hate crimes"—as reported by law-enforcement professionals—declined, but "intimidation," a low-level offense, made up nearly half, (46 percent), of all these crimes in 2006. The FBI defines intimidation as threatening words or other conduct which places an individual in fear of bodily harm, but without actual physical attack.[32] The balance of the crimes against persons in 2006 classified as "hate crimes" were simple assault (31.9 percent) and aggravated assault (21.6 percent). Only three murders and six forcible rapes were reported as "hate crimes."[33]

Set against the so-called epidemic of hate crimes in America are the 11,401,313 total crimes committed against persons or

Just 1,415 of the 9,080 hate crimes reported to the FBI in 2006 were identified as offenses motivated by prejudice against the victim's sexual orientation.

property in 2006.[34] This is compared to the 9,080 "bias motivation" crimes committed in that year.[35] "Hate crimes" account for .08[36] percent of the total crime problem facing America.

But that's not all. Just 1,415 of the 9,080 hate crimes reported to the FBI in 2006 were identified as offenses motivated by prejudice against the victim's sexual orientation.[37] Crimes against homosexuals as an identified class are just .012[38] percent of all crimes committed in America. Despite that, both the House and Senate passed hate crime legislation in 2007 to increase penalties for crimes motivated in some measure by bias against the victim's "sexual orientation." This proposed federal remedy, which has vast and ominous implications for the family and free speech, comes despite the minute number of hate crimes against homosexuals committed each year. Only a veto threat from President George W. Bush kept the measure from becoming law.[39]

The added penalties imposed on hate crimes offenders can be draconian.

Is the Impact Greater?

Actually, crimes of bias or prejudice—which carry more severe penalties—are not any worse in their impact than other crimes. However, the added penalties imposed on hate crime offenders can be draconian. Alabama's hate crime law, for example has a mandatory added sentence of 15 years for felony offenses;[40] Florida's bias crime law triples the maximum penalty applicable for the same offense, but without evidence of hate.[41]

A widely asserted justification for these tougher penalties is that bias crimes "tend to be *excessively brutal*."[42] The Justice Department under the Clinton administration made that charge and asserted that hate crimes "result in more serious injuries than common criminal attacks." That claim, however, is not supported by empirical research. While academics and policymakers regard that claim as a "truism," legal scholar Phyllis B. Gerstenfeld writes, "The truth ... is that there is little empirical evidence to support this claim."[43]

Interest groups and scholars also justify more severe penalties for hate crimes by claiming that bias crimes do greater psychological damage than other crimes. The U.S. Supreme Court itself made that claim in a 1993 opinion by stating, without evidence, that hate crimes are "more likely to . . . inflict distinct emotional harm on their victims."[44]

Again, this claim is not supported by research. A 1994 study found that victims of "hate crimes" do not suffer more than other victims of crime.[45] Paul Aganski, a scholar who has reviewed the literature on this question, calls the findings "equivocal." According to Aganski, "not all of the findings to date conclusively demonstrate a distinct class of psychic injury associated with hate crimes."[46]

An Offense Against Society?

A third reason offered to justify harsher sentences for hate crimes is that bias-motivated crimes hurt innocent third parties. Sociologists Jack Levin and Jack McDevitt claim that "hate crimes are offenses against society. They target not only a primary victim, but everyone in the victim's group—in fact, everyone perceived as different."[47]

However, crimes committed out of bigotry or bias are hardly unique in sending a wave of fear and anxiety through a community. A string of brutal rapes on a college campus will greatly disturb and trouble female students. A series of home invasions will profoundly unsettle residents in a community.

Concern over crime is something shared by all Americans, regardless of their ethnicity or their pattern of sexual behavior.

Not only are bias crimes not a significant national problem, but their effect is no worse than any other assault on person or property. When crimes are committed out of prejudice, the physical, emotional, and social impacts are no greater than those from generic crimes.

In fact, the third-party impact of hate crimes is likely lessened, due to the fact that most crimes classified as hate crimes are low-level offenses. Intimidation and simple assault, as noted above, made up 77.9 percent of all hate crime offenses against persons in 2006.[48]

The Case for Hate Crime Laws Stumbles Badly

When you add up the numbers and examine the impact, the case for hate crime laws stumbles badly. Legal scholar Daniel Troy has stated, "There is little if any evidence that states are not prosecuting all of the crimes that the proponents of such laws want to see prosecuted. And there is no evidence that serious crimes are being ignored."[49]

Hate crime laws are already making

certain viewpoints and beliefs criminal.

But if there is no evidence that hate crime laws are going to punish criminal behavior that is not already being prosecuted, there is plenty of evidence that such laws will increase a dangerous trend toward criminalizing thought. In effect, "hate crime" laws are already making certain viewpoints and beliefs criminal.

TRUTH 3

Hate Crime Laws Criminalize Thought

Blowing whistles and wielding large foam boards, a mob of pink-shirted homosexuals surrounded 11 Christians on a Philadelphia sidewalk in October 2004. The homosexual "Pink Angels" were trying to drown out and hide the Christians from view as they brought the Gospel and God's Word to a large public homosexual gathering called "Outfest." Police soon brought an end to the confrontation, arresting the offenders for disorderly conduct and depositing them in jail, where they spent the next 21 hours.

But it was not the homosexuals who were put behind bars. It was the Christians.

Afterwards, a zealous local prosecutor charged the Christians, who came to be known as the Philadelphia 11, with eight felony and misdemeanor counts, including one count of "ethnic intimidation"—Pennsylvania's term for a hate crime. The charges could have sent the Christians to jail for 47 years and forced them to pay $90,000 in fines.[50]

SURROUNDED: "Pink Angels" encircle Christians from Repent America as they attempt to present the Gospel at a Philadelphia festival for homosexuals in October 2004.

(Repent America)

Ted Hoppe, an attorney for the Christians, called it "the first case in the United States where someone was charged with a hate crime for ministering the Gospel in public."[51]

Assistant District Attorney Charles Ehrlich attacked the Christians not just for what they allegedly did, but for what they said. The Christians had read aloud the Bible's condemnation of homosexuality at the Outfest gathering, uttering what Ehrlich, in a pretrial hearing, called "hateful, disgusting, despicable words."[52]

All charges were later dropped when a Philadelphia County judge cut short prosecutor Ehrlich's attempt to criminalize the words of Scripture. According to Hoppe, the prosecutor was trying to "send a message to these Christian evangelists that if you come down, we're going to make it as painful to you as possible, so stay away."[53]

WARNING: D. James Kennedy warned in 2004 that hate crime laws are "extremely dangerous."

Enforcing Political Correctness

What happened in Philadelphia demonstrates how hate crime laws can be used to chill or silence free speech. They function as a legal tool to enforce political correctness. They empower police and prosecutors to arrest and charge offenders not for what they do, but for what they think and say.

Hate crime laws add penalties to existing statutes when a crime committed is deemed to be motivated in some measure by a bias toward the victim. While such laws may be well-meaning, they give the state the power to police and penalize thought—which is both unconstitutional and a dramatic departure from the American legal tradition.

"The Founding Fathers believed that the law extended to action and not to internal subjective attitudes of people's hearts," said the late Dr. D. James Kennedy, founder of Coral Ridge Ministries. He called hate crime laws "extremely dangerous."[54]

Actions Only—Not Opinions

President Thomas Jefferson offered a concise outline of the American understanding of limited government when he wrote in his famous letter to the Danbury Baptists that "the legitimate powers of government reach actions only, & not opinions. . . ."[55]

The idea that the long arm of the law may not reach beyond actions and assert jurisdiction over the minds of men is the foundation for free speech and religious liberty. It is a unique and precious safeguard to liberty—one rooted in the Bible and worked out in the Reformation. Martin Luther, who risked death at the hands of the state for his opinions, put it this way,

> The temporal lords want to rule the church, and, conversely, the theologians want to play the lord in the town hall. Under the papacy, mixing the two was considered ruling well, and it is still so considered. But in reality this is ruling very badly. . . .[56]

Roger Williams, the founder of Rhode Island, was a Puritan who subscribed to Luther's view. He wrote, "An enforced uniformity of religion throughout a nation or civil state confounds [mixes] the civil and religious, [and] denies the principles of Christianity."[57]

LIMITED: Thomas Jefferson said "the legitimate powers of government reach actions only, & not opinions...."
(Library of Congress)

God Is Lord of the Conscience

The Westminster Confession, an authoritative statement of Reformation belief embraced by Puritan New England, declared that "God alone is Lord of the conscience, and hath left it free from the doctrines and commandments of men which are in any thing contrary to his Word....[58]

This idea found political expression in the 1786 Virginia Act for Establishing Religious Freedom, which abolished legal requirements to attend and support the established church. The Act declared that "Almighty God hath created the mind free" and drew up a formula for freedom taken from the life of Jesus Christ. Civil mandates over religious belief, the Act states, "are a departure from the plan of the Holy Author of our religion, who being Lord both of body and mind, yet chose not to propagate it by coercions on either, as was in his Almighty power to do."[59]

GOD-GIVEN: Individual conscience is "beyond the reach of any human power," according to Supreme Court Justice Joseph Story.
(Library of Congress)

Supreme Court Justice Joseph Story restated the sanctity of individual conscience when he declared in his 1833 *Commentaries on the U.S. Constitution,*

> The rights of conscience are, indeed, beyond the reach of any human power. They are given by God, and cannot be encroached upon by human authority, without a criminal disobedience of the precepts of natural, as well as of revealed religion.[60]

Courts Support Liberty of Conscience

Liberty of conscience has been long upheld by American courts. The U.S. Supreme Court declared in 1929,

> If there is any principle of the Constitution that more imperatively calls for attachment than any other, it is the principle of free thought—not free thought for those who agree with us, but freedom for the thought we hate.[61]

The High Court came back to that principle in 1989, when it ruled that,

> If there is a bedrock principle underlying the First Amendment, it is that the government may not prohibit the expression of an idea simply because society finds the idea itself offensive or disagreeable.[62]

Hate Crime Laws Punish Ideas

But that constitutional bedrock is imperiled by hate crime laws. Wendy Kaminer is a civil libertarian and former American Civil Liberties Union board member who opposes bias crime laws. "Hate crime legislation ...," she has written, "is expressly designed to punish particular thoughts or ideas."[63]

The Ohio Supreme Court agreed with the position, striking down a state hate crime law in 1992. The court warned that "if the legislature can enhance a penalty for crimes committed 'by reason of' racial bigotry, why not 'by reason of' opposition to abortion, war, the elderly (or any other political viewpoint)?"[64]

One viewpoint for which Christians, such as the Philadelphia 11, could be sent to jail is opposition to homosexual conduct. Such opposition may be classified as a hate crime if legislation to add "sexual orientation" to the federal hate crimes statute becomes law. The Alliance Defense Fund has warned that such legislation may subject "politically incorrect speech to federal prosecution."[65] The measure defines "intimidation"—a term encompassing both speech and action—as violence. It could empower federal prosecutors to charge the proclamation of God's Word regarding homosexual conduct—even from the pulpit—as a hate crime.

"The reality is that so-called hate crime laws are designed to punish people for what they think, feel, or believe," said ADF Senior Counsel Glen Lavy. "Violent crimes should be punished regardless of the characteristics of the victim. 'Hate crime' laws are an effort to enforce the orthodoxy of political correctness and to curtail freedom of speech."

The result of these laws is not greater justice, but unequal justice.

TRUTH 4

Hate Crime Laws Violate Equal Justice Under the Law

He picked the wrong victims. David Wyant and his wife were at an Ohio state park in 1989 with their music turned up loud. After a black couple at a nearby campsite complained to park staff, Wyant turned off his tunes.

But about 15 minutes later the radio came back on and Wyant uncorked his anger, shouting a harsh and ugly remark within earshot of the black couple. "We didn't have this problem until those n——- moved in next to us," Wyant said. "I ought to shoot that black motherf——-. I ought to kick his black a—."

For that, Ohio convicted Wyant of ethnic intimidation—a hate crime and a fourth-degree felony, and sent him to prison for 18 months. The sentence was *three times* the maximum length he would have faced for the basic offense of aggravated menacing. If his victims had been white, he would have been charged with a first degree misdemeanor and faced jail time of 0-6 months or a fine.[66]

A Two-Tiered System

Wyant's conviction—he lost on appeal all the way up to the U.S. Supreme Court—displays how hate crime laws create a two-tiered system of justice. Instead of equal justice under law, hate crime statutes impose more severe penalties when the victims belong to certain specially protected groups. The same crime brings different time—depending on the victims.

Front of U.S. Supreme Court building. 

Lady Justice is no longer an impartial arbiter of justice. Now she lifts her blindfold to peek at the skin color, ethnicity, gender, religion, and, in some states, the "sexual orientation" of the victim. Hate crime laws tip the scales of justice in favor of people from these protected groups—and no others.

That doesn't sit well with many. The West Virginia Troopers Association asked their state legislature in 2001 to repeal its hate crime law. "We as police officers want to treat everybody equally. I don't think the public would expect us to distinguish between a black person or a white one or a handicapped person or a nonhandicapped, gay or non-gay," association executive director David Moye said in explaining the unusual demand.[67]

Unequal Punishments

But hate crime laws offend not just West Virginia state troopers; they insult traditional American notions about equal justice. They also mark a return to the system of unequal justice that prevailed under the Code of Hammurabi seventeen centuries before Christ.[68] The Code, like modern hate crime laws, called for

varying punishments, depending not just on the nature of the offense but on the status of the offended. For example:

> If any one strike the body of a man higher in rank than he, he shall receive sixty blows with an ox-whip in public.
>
> If a free-born man strike the body of another free-born man or equal rank, he shall pay one gold mina.
>
> If the slave of a freed man strike the body of a freed man, his ear shall be cut off.

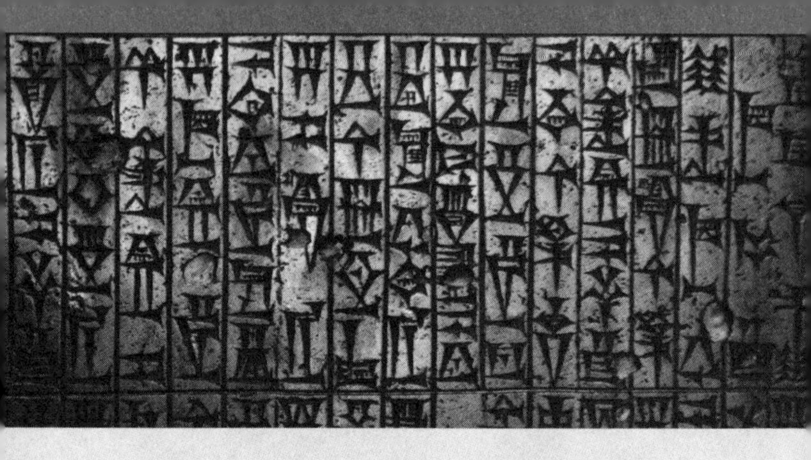

UNEQUAL JUSTICE: Detail from Code of Hammurabi inscribed on stone slab.

The practical effect of this system of varying punishments was, as legal scholar Daniel Troy has pointed out, to reinforce "a rigid caste system"—an outcome we will also see in America, if ideological law prevails.[69]

God Has One Standard for All

Unlike Hammurabi's Code, Old Testament law called for equal justice, without respect to persons. The law God gave to Moses made it abundantly clear that one standard of justice was to apply to all. Moses told the ancient Israelites:

IMPARTIAL: God's law, given to Moses, applied one standard of justice to all.
(Library of Congress)

You shall do no injustice in judgment. You shall not be partial to the poor, nor honor the person of the mighty. In righteousness you shall judge your neighbor."

—Leviticus 19:15

You shall not show partiality to a poor man in his dispute.

—Exodus 23:3

You shall not show partiality in judgment; you shall hear the small as well as the great; you shall not be afraid in any man's presence, for the judgment is God's.

—Deuteronomy 1:16-17

True Justice Reflects God's Character

Blind justice, introduced some 3,500 years ago in the law of Moses, is a requirement based on the character of God Himself.

For the Lord your God is God of gods and Lord of lords, the great God, mighty and awesome, who shows no partiality nor takes a bribe.

—Deuteronomy 10:17

Western law, based largely on the Judeo-Christian legal tradition, has progressively applied the principle of equality before the law. While the United States has not always lived up to that standard, its founding document, the Declaration of Independence, states that "all men are created equal and endowed by their Creator with certain unalienable rights…."

This powerful phrase was not "merely political rhetoric," according to legal scholar Herbert W. Titus, "but was a deliberate endorsement of a political philosophy that would ultimately destroy special privileges in the New World."[70]

The Constitution Bans Special Rights

Some of those special privileges were part of the common law inherited from Britain. American statesmen, Titus writes, set about to purge this body of British law of its "special royal and ecclesiastical privileges."[71] American distaste for special rights accounts for the ban in the U.S. Constitution on titles of nobility, a departure from the European habit of privileging the aristocracy above commoners.

State constitutions also included provisions to remove special rights from the common law. The Oregon constitution, for example, included this provision,

No law shall be passed granting to any citizen or class of citizens privileges, or immunities, which, upon the same terms, shall not equally belong to all citizens.[72]

The Fourteenth Amendment sought to correct the Founders' decision to exclude African Americans from the full protection of the law. It affirms, as the U.S. Supreme Court declared in 1879, "that all persons, whether colored or white, shall stand equal before the laws of the States...."[73]

All Citizens Are Equal Before the Law

Always honored, equality before the law was not always practiced, as in 1896, when the U.S. Supreme Court, to its shame, upheld a Louisiana law mandating the separation of black from white Americans. Justice John Marshall Harlan offered a lonely but powerful dissent,

There is no caste here. Our constitution is color-blind, and neither knows nor tolerates classes among citizens. In respect of civil rights, all citizens are equal before the law. The humblest is the peer of the most powerful. The law regards man as man, and takes no account of his surroundings or of his color when his civil rights as guaranteed by the supreme law of the land are involved.[74]

BLIND JUSTICE: Supreme Court Justice John Marshall Harlan said the Constitution does not tolerate "classes among citizens."
(Library of Congress)

But under the hate crimes regime, the law no longer regards "man as man," but as a member of a group. Equal justice gives way to a system of "preferential justice," in which, as novelist George Orwell put it, "All animals are equal, but some animals are more equal than others."[75]

Fragmenting American Society

That didn't work for the *Animal Farm*, and it will not work for the United States either. Hate crime laws favor designated groups and will lead to the fragmentation of American society.

When that happens, watch out. If justice is dispensed according to group membership, competing factions will have the power to use civil law to advance their own interests—at the expense of equal justice for all.

Some, however, are quite willing for this to happen; if it will advance their desired social agenda.

TRUTH 5

Hate Crime Laws Are About Recognition, Not Fighting Crime

When it comes to hate crimes, some victim groups are more equal than others. Some qualify for added protection; some do not.

That became painfully evident in 2007 when the U.S. House of Representatives Judiciary Committee took up a series of Republican amendments crafted to broaden the number of groups protected under a hate crime bill before Congress. One by one, amendments to protect seven at-risk groups were offered and, one by one, they were defeated on party-line votes.

Unborn children, members of the Armed Forces, senior citizens, pregnant women, witnesses in a judicial proceeding, victims of prior crimes, and children were all rejected for inclusion in the "Local Law Enforcement Hate Crimes Prevention Act of 2007." Only victims attacked because of their "actual or perceived race, color, religion, national origin, gender, sexual orientation, gender identity, or disability" qualified to be protected under the bill.[76] And that is by design.

An Instrument of Social Policy

The fact that just a short list of preferred victims is included in the federal hate crime bill lays bare the true purpose behind anti-bias laws. The point is not to protect bias-crime victims nor, frankly, is there a need to, since laws already exist to punish crime, whether motivated by prejudice or not. The real purpose is social engineering—to instruct the public on which prejudices are proscribed and which may be safely indulged.

This is particularly true with respect to homosexuals who, for the first time, are included in a hate crime measure that was passed in 2007 by both the House and Senate, but failed to become law after President George W. Bush issued a veto threat.[77] If this or similar legislation becomes law, it will provide homosexual interest groups with enormous leverage to push for further legal recognition, including the right to marry.

Bias crime laws are very much an instrument of social policy. They "extend the drive against prejudice to matters of crime and punishment," write James B. Jacobs and Kimberly Potter, authors of *Hate Crimes: Criminal Law and Identity Politics*.[78] They are enacted, the authors state, for "essentially symbolic reasons."[79]

Grander Purpose

Pronouncements by politicians illustrate the point. In 1990, New Jersey Governor Jim Florio suggested a much grander purpose for a hate crime bill under consideration in the Garden state than simply locking up offenders,

> **This legislation [ethnic intimidation law] does more than punish . . . . It says something about who we are, and about the ideals to which this state is committed.**[80]

REJECTED: Capitol Hill lawmakers turned down efforts to give seven at-risk groups federal hate crimes protection.

New York Governor Mario Cuomo cast the purpose of a hate crime measure in much the same terms in a letter to state legislators,

[Our] single most effective weapon is the law. I implore you to support the Bias Related Violence and Intimidation Act I have proposed, and make it clear to the people of this state that behavior based on bias will not be ignored or tolerated.[81]

In 2000, Georgia state representative Dan Ponder, Jr. urged his colleagues to vote for a hate crime measure in a speech that included a remarkably frank confession that fighting crime was not the true issue,

> I would say to you that now is our turn to send a message. I am not a lawyer, I don't know how difficult it would be to prosecute this or even care. I don't really care that anyone is ever prosecuted under this bill. But I do care that we take this moment in time, in history, to say that we are going to send a message.[82]

Sending a Message

Sending a message was the primary purpose in 1990 of the federal "Hate Crimes Statistics Act." That law called on the Justice Department to collect statistics on the commission of crimes that "manifest evidence of prejudice based on race, religion, sexual orientation, or ethnicity."

It was touted as an aid to law enforcement, a tool to raise public awareness about hate crimes, and a declaration that the federal government takes hate crimes seriously. While the information gathered about hate crimes has been of limited value to law enforcement, due to incomplete reporting from the states and the use of varying definitions of what constitutes a hate crime, the HCSA sends a powerful message.

That was the hope of Joan Weiss, then-executive director of the National Institute Against Prejudice and Violence. "It will take many years of national reporting before we have a meaningful data base," she said in 1989. "But we need to start right away so Americans realize we have a serious problem with hate crimes."[83]

No Women or Children

The symbolic value of hate crime legislation is illustrated by two groups left out of the Hate Crimes Statistics Act's list of protected categories: women and children. The coalition of Jewish, black, homosexual, ethnic, and nationality groups lobbying for passage of the Hate Crimes Statistics Act opposed adding gender for a curious reason. As Jacobs and Potter point out,

> [M]isogynistic violence against women is so prevalent, its inclusion would overwhelm the other species of hate crime. In other words, at this symbolic level, groups perceive themselves to be in competition with one another for attention.[84]

The exclusion of children is striking. There are some three million reports of child abuse every year[85] and, as the authors of *Hate Crimes: Criminal Law and Identity Politics* suggest, some percentage of attacks on children must be related to prejudice. "Nothing," they write, "could more poignantly demonstrate what we mean by 'the social construction of hate crime'"[86] than the exclusion of children from the HCSA roster of protected groups.

"Protected Group" Status Is What Counts

The absence of women as a protected group under the HCSA angered feminists. Molly Yard, then-president of the National Organization for Women told a congressional hearing that gathering national data on incidences of rape and domestic violence is not enough.

[C]ategorization of such crimes as hate crimes is necessary in order for law enforcement personnel, legislators, educators, and the public at large to truly understand not just the full scope and complexity of the problem, but the motivation behind these crimes.[87]

More important, it seems, than the actual crime data, which was already being collected, was the designation of women as hate crime victims.

But while women and children lost out in the grievance sweepstakes, homosexuals won the jackpot. The HCSA was, as the National Gay and Lesbian Task Force proclaims on its website, "the first federal statute in our country's history that named and recognized lesbian, gay and bisexual people."[88]

And, after all, recognition—not fighting crime—is what it is all about. However, for those who are concerned with fighting crime, as well as for law enforcement officials, the task of identifying and prosecuting hate crimes is great indeed.

TRUTH 6

Hate Crime Laws Burden the Justice System

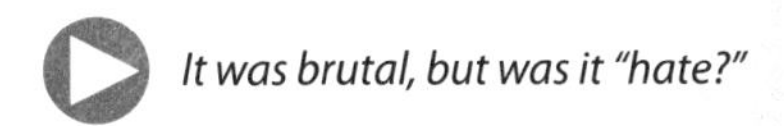

Eighteen-year-old Stephen Moller smashed Sean Kennedy's face with his fist in May 2007, sending Kennedy, 20, onto the pavement outside a Greenville, South Carolina, liquor establishment. Moller, who had been out drinking with friends that night, drove off with his friends, but shortly afterward left a mocking voice mail with a woman who was with Kennedy, "You tell your faggot friend that when he wakes up, he owes me $500 for my broken hand.'"[89]

Kennedy died within a day from the vicious punch, which police initially determined came as "a result of the defendant not liking the sexual identity of the victim."[90] A police investigator later pieced together the events that led to the assault and testified in court that Mellor found out only after he drove away that his victim was a homosexual.[91]

Kennedy's mother[92] and homosexual activists reject that conclusion and have called on South Carolina legislators to pass a state hate crime law.[93]

Divining the Mind of the Accused

The lingering and passionate dispute over whether and how much prejudice inflamed Moller's mind when he threw his fatal blow showcases the burden placed on police by hate crime laws. It's not enough to find, arrest, and charge the culprit. Much more is required. Police must divine the presence of bias and then determine if enough ugly attitude exists to elevate a garden variety crime into a "hate" offense.

It's not an easy task. That's because the entire "hate crimes" concept is hopelessly subjective and "loaded with ambiguity," as Jacobs and Potter point out.[94] Hate crime laws require law enforcement officials not only to define "prejudice," but to determine which prejudices are outlawed when linked to a particular crime. Prosecutors must also determine whether a strong enough "causal link" connects the offender's prejudice with his crime.

How Much Hate Must Be Present?

All this, writes John Leo, "gets courts into a maelstrom.... Why should courts be in the business of judging these misty matters?"[95]

Police may be muttering that question to themselves as they try to calculate the hate quotient in a crime. A federal hate crime is defined as an offense "motivated, *in whole or in part*, by the offender's bias against a race, religion, disability, sexual orientation, or ethnicity/national origin."[96] But "in whole or in part" leaves unanswered the question of how much hate must be present to trigger a hate crime sentence enhancement.

The FBI, in its attempt to give guidance to law enforcement professionals on how to count hate crimes, acknowledge the murky nature of the whole enterprise.

The mere fact that the offender is biased against the victim's race, religion, disability, sexual orientation, and/or ethnicity/national origin does not mean that a hate crime was involved. Rather, the offender's criminal act must have been motivated, in whole or in part, by his/her bias. Because motivation is subjective, it is difficult to know with certainty whether a crime was the result of the offender's bias.[97]

The fuzzy and subjective nature of hate crime designations opens the door for interest groups to pressure police as they investigate an offense and determine if it should be labeled a "hate crime." That labeling decision, Jacobs and Potter write, is "fraught with sensitive, even potentially explosive, social and political ramifications."[98]

Passions Run High

Passions run high over these matters. A defense attorney complained in 2005 about the "public frenzy" whipped up after six suspects beat a young homosexual man. New Mexico governor Bill Richardson participated in a candlelight vigil for the victim and called for the suspects to be given the maximum penalties possible under the state's hate crime law. The case, the attorney said, was "being politicized to the point of frenzy."[99]

When a man described as "black/Hispanic" beat up and hospitalized a Korea-American grocery store owner on Staten Island in 1992, police said it was not a hate crime. That did not sit well with New York's Human Rights Commissioner, who arrived at the store with media in tow to condemn what he called the "alarming increase in bias incidents on Staten Island." Staten Island borough president Guy Molinari rejected the charge and asserted that "there is a larger crime being committed with increasing frequency in our city, the crime of fomenting exaggerated fears."[100]

Public uproar in 1992 over a series of incidents that carried racial overtones, according to many, and even the *New York Times* reminded its readers that not every attack is motivated by "hate." The *Times* took issue with police designation of a robbery as a hate crime and cautioned "everyone—political leaders, the media, the police and the public—to avoid hasty generalizations that make the bad even worse."[101]

Probing for Bias

But the bad does get worse at trial when prosecutors try to prove the presence of hate. Doing so often requires intrusive questions into the mind and motivation of the offender—questions that under other circumstances would be judged irrelevant to determining the defendant's actual guilt or innocence.

A San Francisco prosecutor probed in 2004 for bias in a white teenager charged with a hate crime. The 17-year-old boy had joined other young white males in attacking five Asian American teenagers. The prosecutor wanted to know whether the teen had ever used the term "Chinaman,"

He denied saying "Chinaman" that night, but said he has in the past. "I do not know one person who hasn't said 'Chinaman,'" he testified under cross-examination. He later clarified: "I've said 'Chinaman,' but not in a racist form. If you call someone a Frenchman, or Italianman, it's not offensive."[102]

That foray into the mind of the teen pales before an Ohio prosecutor's attempt to show racial bigotry in David Wyant, who was charged in 1989 with an interracial hate offense. The prosecutor wanted to know about his relationship with his black neighbor,

Q: And you lived next door to [a 65-year-old black neighbor of the defendant's] for nine years and you don't even know her first name?

A: No.

Q: Never had dinner with her?

A: No.

Q: Never gone out and had a beer with her?

A: No.

Q: Never went to a movie?

A: No.

Q: Never invited her to a picnic at your house?

A: No.

Q: Never invited her to Alum Creek

A: No. She never invited me nowhere.

Q: You don't associate with her, do you?

A: I talk with her when I can, whenever I see her out.

Q: All these black people that you have described that are your friends, I want you to give me one person, just one who was really a good friend of yours.[103]

Burdening the Justice System

Hate crimes laws are a burden and distraction to the justice system. They divert time, energy, and attention away from "really important things," as Philadelphia Mayor Michael Nutter acknowledged when asked about a two-year investigation by the Philadelphia Commission on Human Rights.

After looking into whether a restaurant had transgressed by posting a sign telling patrons to speak English, the commission finally dismissed the complaint, and Nutter was asked if the inquiry had been appropriate. "I think that based on the role and mission of the Human Relations Commission, which is to work on these kinds of issues, it's appropriate for them to have taken that action," he said. "At some point in time, we'll all go back to our lives and try to work on really important things, like lowering the crime rate, getting kids in school, creating jobs and cleaning up the corruption in the city."[104]

Hate crime laws are a burden and distraction to the justice system.

They divert time, energy, and attention away from "really important things."

— Philadelphia Mayor Michael Nutter

But purging the nation of prejudice comes first, according to social engineers. Doing so, however, pits group against group, and divides America into feuding factions.

TRUTH 7

Hate Crime Laws Are a Vehicle for Identity Politics

Hyman Kaplan would not approve. For Kaplan, the indominitable, albeit English-challenged immigrant immortalized by writer Leo C. Rosten, the goal was to become an American. Rosten's fictional character never overcame his propensity to mangle English, what he called a "sleeping of the tong," but he was resolute in his desire to adopt the ways of his new country. As he put it, "I said to minesalf, 'Keplen, you in America, so tink like de Americans *tink!'"*[105]

That attitude no longer prevails. "Important pockets of new American immigrants are not assimilating, not learning English, not becoming or thinking of themselves primarily as Americans," writes social commentator Roger Kimball.[106] American education may have something to do with this. Sociologists Alejandro Portes and Ruben Rumbaut reported in 2001 that four years in an American high school left immigrant youth less likely, not more, to regard themselves as Americans.[107] But as the authors of the recently published *Bradley Project on America's National Identity* state, "This is not their fault; it is ours."[108]

Tribalism in America

Not just some immigrants, but even native-born Americans are identifying themselves as members of an ethnic, national, or racial category first and foremost. What some would call "the Balkanization of America," is being swept forward and supported by so-called hate crime legislation.

Hate crime statutes codify legal distinctions based on race, ethnicity, national origin, gender, and sexual behavior. They alert all Americans to these distinct identities and reinforce, magnify, and fix in place group conflict by using the law to make them legitimate. The media reinforce these divisions by showering attention on crimes purported to be motivated by prejudice.

Clearly, hate crime laws are a vehicle for "identity politics"—a state of affairs in which individuals see themselves as members of factions that are competing for special privileges and positions in American society. Based on differences in race, gender, religion, or sexual conduct, such factionalism is moving our society toward the "disuniting of America." Some are calling this a "new tribalism."

"We've moved from 'we, the people,' to 'we, the peoples,'" according to the Bradley Foundation report.[109] Multiculturalism and the ideals of diversity have replaced once commonly held assumptions about what it means to be an American. A 2008 poll commissioned for the Bradley Foundation found that while 84 percent of respondents believe in a unique American identity, 63 percent think this common identity is weakening. Twenty-four percent think our divisions have advanced past the point of a return to a broadly shared national identity.

NEW GOSPEL: Scholar Arthur Schlesinger, Jr. warned about the new "ethnic gospel" of multiculturalism which "nourishes prejudices."

A New Ethnic Gospel

Liberal scholar Arthur Schlesinger warned about all this in 1992 in his book, *The Disuniting of America*. According to Schlesinger,

> The new ethnic gospel rejects the unifying vision of individuals from all nations melted into a new race. Its underlying philosophy is that America is not a nation of individuals at all, but a nation of groups....[110]

This "separatism," Schlesinger writes, comes at a cost. It "nourishes prejudices, magnifies differences, and stirs antagonisms."[111]

Hate crime laws expedite the process of disuniting by harnessing the power of the law. When the law exalts group identities and grants special status to victims based on their membership in certain privileged groups, justice becomes the right of a few. This is very much like the legal circumstances under the Code of Hammurabi where justice was apportioned on the basis of social status and served to sustain a caste system.

A Return to the Medieval Period

Hate crime laws are a return to the medieval period, "which was based upon status, caste and privilege," according to Morgan Reynolds, Director of the Criminal Justice Center at the National Center for Policy Analysis. Medieval criminal penalties, he writes, varied, based on the victim's status.[111]

MELTING POT: The instrument of equal rights is the means to ethnic assimilation in this 1889 cartoon from Puck *magazine.*

Hate crime laws are a return to the medieval period,

"which was based upon status, caste and privilege,"

— Morgan Reynolds

Bias crime legislation also shares traits with pre-Christian law in England, where the clan, not the man, took precedence in the law. Under this system, as Attorney Daniel Troy explains, "A murder was regarded as an affront to the clan, not to the individual murdered. Recompense took place among groups."[112] It was the influence of Christianity that brought a shift in view, and as Troy stated, "punishment came to be assessed without regard to the status of the victim within the group."[113]

Hate crime laws reverse this. They make group status a salient factor in the administration of justice and "ultimately erode the core unifying values of our country," as Troy points out.[114] For example, the addition of "sexual orientation," greatly offends Christians and conservative Jews.[115] This term presumes a fixed identity for those who, as a matter of choice, engage in same-gender sex. The Bible calls such behavior "sodomy," and condemns it. Giving special protection under the law to homosexuals by including "sexual orientation" as a protected category in hate crime laws serves as a flashpoint for social conflict and is an assault on the values of America's civic culture.

Victimhood Brings Political Power

Hate crime legislation also creates a perverse incentive to seek victimhood, since victimization enhances a group's "moral claim on the larger society"[116] and, therefore, it leverages political power. Interest groups that claim to represent racial minorities, women, or homosexuals, have a vested interest in gaining special status under hate crime laws. Ironically, victimhood is a path to power. As Shelby Steele writes, "The power to be found in victimization, like any power, is intoxicating and can lend itself to the creation of a new class of super-victims who can feel the pea of victimization under twenty mattresses."

The special power of the victim to command attention and social benefits is traceable to the 1960s when, as Charles Sykes writes, "the political and moral stature of the victim was transformed and made attractive to an increasingly wide array of groups" seeking access to an "elaborate array of programs, privileges, and entitlements that were specifically attached to various groups' victim status."[117]

But social tensions ensue when the logic of affirmative action works its way into criminal law. The law gives rise to conflict when it grants special status, "special protections and special handouts"[118] to groups which claim the status of victims.

Balkanization

Another perverse outcome of hate crime laws is to transform concern over crime, typically a source of social cohesion, into a cause of social friction. "It reinforces differences rather than uniting us all, regardless of identity, into Americans who are together repulsed by crime."[119]

America was uniquely founded on a set of ideas, not an ethnic identity. As the French-born farmer, Hector St. John de Crevecoeur, said in 1782 of his adopted nation, America is a place where we leave behind all "ancient prejudices and manners," and "are melted into a new race of men."[120]

Balkan countries of Europe, where identity politics prevailed, went through four stages on the road to disaster:

"ethnic awareness, separatism, mysticism, and cleansing." The first three stages are pushed along by hate crime laws.

— Morgan Reynolds

But hate crime laws are beginning to undo that American experience and transplant ancient enmities, as well as introduce new ones. "Down this road, of course, ultimately lies disaster," writes Morgan Reynolds. He points out that the Balkan countries of Europe, where identity politics prevailed, went through four stages on the road to disaster: "ethnic awareness, separatism, mysticism, and cleansing." The first three stages, he writes, are pushed along by hate crime laws.[121]

The movement to recognize aggrieved groups in the law is alien to the American idea and will only advance the Balkanization already taking place in our land. It serves to make many of one.

WEAKENING: Sixty-three percent of Americans think our nation's common identity is weakening, according to a poll for the Bradley Foundation.

As the Bradley Foundation warned in its own recent *E Pluribus Unum* report, "We should not adopt policies that perpetuate division or that compromise our national allegiance."[122]

Such policies have already been adopted outside our borders, and the consequences have been chilling.

TRUTH 8

Hate Crime Laws Jeopardize Freedom of Speech

Anyone who thinks hate crime laws are a good idea here in the U.S. should take careful note of their impact in other countries, where no First Amendment exists to safeguard freedoms of speech and religion.

Incidents in four Western nations—Sweden, Australia, Britain, and Canada—send a chilling warning to Americans. They clearly show how hate crime laws are colliding with liberty and religious freedom.

Horrors Beyond Our Borders

Burdened with "deep sorrow" over how homosexuality had "engulfed our society," Ake Green knew he had to speak out. It did not matter to him that the penalty under Swedish law for expressions of disrespect toward homosexuals is up to four years in prison.

He told his small congregation in Borgholm, Sweden, in 2003 that homosexuality is "a deep cancerous tumor in the entire society" and "an evil force." He also offered "abundant grace," to those "who live under the slavery of sexual immorality."[123]

INDICTED: Swedish authorities charged Pastor Ake Green with a hate crime after he preached a sermon declaring the Bible's verdict on homosexual conduct.
(Alliance Defense Fund)

A prosecutor read Green's sermon in a local newspaper and charged Green with disrespect toward homosexuals. "One may have whatever religion one wishes, but this is an attack on all fronts against homosexuals," prosecutor Kjell Yngvesson said. "Collecting Bible citations on this topic as he (Green) does makes this hate speech."[124]

A district court agreed and sentenced Green in 2004 to one month in prison.

Preachers "As Criminals"

"I am not a criminal," Green said at the time. "I don't feel like a criminal, but this new law makes us preachers 'as criminals' if we speak up."[125]

When Green appealed, the prosecutor argued that his sentence should be lengthened to six months or more. Sweden's leading homosexual rights group, RSFL, agreed. "Hatred and defamation is [are] not to be accepted, just because it's [they're] based on religious beliefs or religious scriptures," an RSFL spokesman said.[126]

> "I am not a criminal, I don't feel like a criminal, **but this new law makes us preachers 'as criminals' if we speak up."**
>
> **—Pastor Ake Green**

An appeals court acquitted Green on February 11, 2005, ruling that his sermon was not "incitement" against homosexuals, but a sermon faithful to the Bible, which he had a right to preach. The Swedish Supreme Court agreed, clearing Green in a unanimous ruling on November 29, 2005.[127]

"Together, with the help of God, we won the battle, and my case is now known in courts across Europe," Pastor Green told the Alliance Defense Fund, which provided legal aid. "We won the battle, but the war is far from over."[128]

Thought Crimes Down Under

While Pastor Green was fending off the thought police in Sweden, two pastors in Australia faced a similar challenge from Muslim accusers.

The two evangelical ministers, Danny Nalliah and Daniel Scot, were accused of vilifying Islam, after a 2002 seminar on Islam taught by Scot at Nalliah's invitation. More than 200 people attended the event—held inside a church—at which Scot explained Islamic beliefs and urged his audience to reach out to Muslims in Christian love.

Three people linked to the Islamic Council of Victoria were also in attendance and later brought complaints under Victoria's Racial and Religious Tolerance Act, a 2001 law that makes it a crime to incite hatred toward a person or a group. A court convicted Scot and Nalliah in December 2004 and ordered them to publish an apology—written by the judge—in their newsletter and website, and pay for eight apology "advertisements" in two newspapers.[129] They were also ordered to never repeat their views about Islam in public.[130]

SILENCED: Danny Nalliah (pictured) and Daniel Scot were charged with vilifying Islam after they gave a seminar on Muslim beliefs inside a church.

Both men refused and appealed the ruling. As Nalliah later told Coral Ridge Ministries' 2007 Reclaiming America for Christ conference, "I said, "No, I will not apologize. I'll go to prison for not apologizing and speaking the truth."[131]

The Supreme Court of Victoria vacated the lower court ruling in December 2006, and the Islamic Council, which was ordered to pay half the pastors' legal fees for the appeal, dropped its lawsuit seven months later.[132]

"The Pastors' commitment to conscience was literally put on trial, but they stood firm and won," said Roger Severino, an attorney for the Becket Fund, which assisted the pastors in court.[133]

The Chilly British Legal Climate

In Britain, a street preacher, elderly pensioners, a bishop, and a member of parliament have all been forced to answer to the law after speaking publicly against homosexual conduct.

Police arrested street preacher Harry Hammond, 69, in 2001, after a mob attacked him because he held a sign reading, "Stop Immorality, Stop Homosexuality, Stop Lesbianism, Jesus is Lord."[134] The protesters wrestled him to the ground, threw dirt, and poured water on him, but the arresting officer blamed Hammond for disrupting public order by opposing homosexuality.[135] A court fined him £300 plus £395 costs,[136] ruling that his sign was insulting, because it linked homosexuality with immorality.[137]

Police interrogated a retired couple, Joe and Helen Roberts, for over an hour in 2005 after they complained to their town council about its pro-homosexual policy.[138] The Roberts said that the officers warned them that they "were close to a hate crime" and were "walking on eggshells."[139]

Police investigated the Bishop of Chester in 2003, after he said that homosexuals could "reorientate themselves" with medical help.[140] That sparked a complaint and a visit from police, who "consulted at length" with prosecutors before determining that no crime had been committed.[141]

Police in Northern Ireland said they were investigating a June 2008 complaint against Iris Robinson, a Member of Parliament, after she said on BBC Radio that the Bible calls homosexuality an "abomination."[142]

The British legal climate is now chilly enough that many Christians contact the Christian Institute, an evangelical advocacy group, because they "fear censure if they express their orthodox Christian beliefs on homosexuality."[143]

The Same Chill in Canada

The same chill has settled over Canada, where it is a crime punishable by up to two years in prison to "incite" or "promote hatred" against protected groups such as homosexuals or Muslims.[144]

Youth pastor Stephen Boissoin sent a letter to his local newspaper in 2002 in which he criticized homosexual activists, but offered compassion for people enslaved by same-sex desires.[145] A reader complained to the Alberta Human Rights Commission, which ordered Boissoin to pay $5,000 to his accuser, who was not even mentioned in the letter. The commission also ordered Boissoin to apologize and

FINED: A human rights commission fined Stephen Boissoin $5,000 after he criticized homosexual activists in a newspaper.

CHARGED: Muslims charged that a Mark Steyn article injured their "dignity, feelings and self-respect." 

banned him from publishing any future "disparaging remarks" about homosexuals.[146]

He is appealing the ruling. "I should have the equal right to freedom of speech in Canada," Boissoin said. "Right now, myself and Christians at large do not have that right."[147]

Free Speech Is Being Throttled

British Columbia's Human Rights Tribunal forced a Canadian newsmagazine to answer for its alleged editorial sins in a weeklong "trial" in June 2008. The tribunal hauled *Macleans*, a leading news publication, into the dock after it published writer Mark Steyn's lengthy warning about the coming Islamization of

Europe. An offended Muslim group asked the tribunal to order *Macleans* to print a rebuttal and pay for the alleged injury to the "dignity, feelings and self-respect" of Muslims.

No verdict had been rendered in the British Columbia matter as of this writing, but the Canadian Human Rights Commission, which heard the same complaint, dismissed all charges against *Macleans*. That surprising decision—the first time in 31 years that Canada's human rights commission has ruled a defendant innocent—came in the wake of intense media scrutiny and a growing awareness among politicians that hate crime laws are throttling free speech in Canada.

That awareness has not yet dawned on America's elected leaders, who continue to press for hate crime legislation that could put our freedom of speech in jeopardy.

TRUTH 9

Hate Crime Laws Threaten Religious Liberty

Rep. Mike Pence (IN) wanted to make it absolutely clear. Knowing that a hate crime law had already been used to attack religious freedom, the talk-host turned legislator asked his House colleagues in 2007 to amend a hate crimes measure so there would be no question as to whether it limits "the religious freedom of any person or group under the Constitution."[148]

Pence reminded fellow members of the House Judiciary Committee that 11 Christians had already been charged under Pennsylvania's hate crime law after holding signs and reading Scripture at a homosexual street festival in Philadelphia.

"The road we could be led down," Pence said, "is one on which pastors, religious broadcasters and evangelical leaders who are speaking their own personal convictions could be prosecuted under hate crimes statutes."[149]

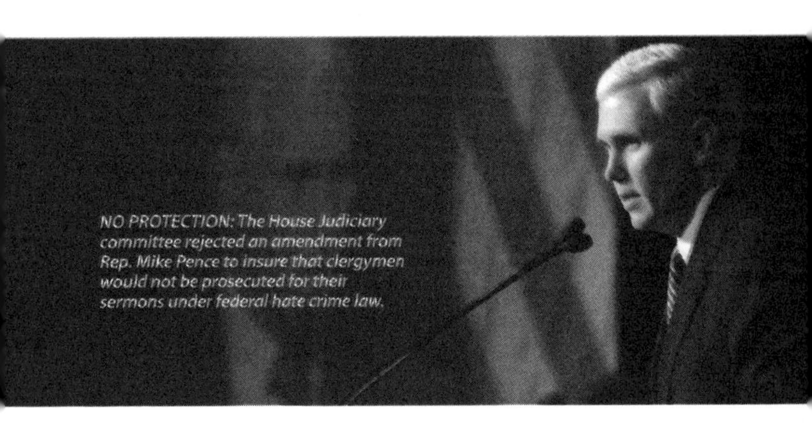

NO PROTECTION: The House Judiciary committee rejected an amendment from Rep. Mike Pence to insure that clergymen would not be prosecuted for their sermons under federal hate crime law.

MUZZLE: Bishop Harry R. Jackson, Jr. warned that hate crime laws can "muzzle the black church." 

No matter. The committee defeated Pence's religious liberty amendment on a straight party-line vote. In so doing, it has set the stage for a collision between hate crime laws and religious liberty.

There's a Train [Wreck] a' Coming

The amendment vote led Alan Sears, Alliance Defense Fund president and a former federal prosecutor, to say that "it could soon be less of a crime to beat up a pregnant woman than it is to criticize homosexual behavior from a pulpit."[150]

A coalition of African-American pastors voiced concern that a federal hate crime law would silence their pulpits. Bishop Harry R. Jackson Jr., founder of the High Impact Leader Coalition, said the measure "can muzzle the black church" and "keep the church from preaching the Gospel."[151]

That sounds overblown, but isn't. Hate crime laws have already been used to ensnare pastors overseas (see chapter 8), while

anti-discrimination codes and other civil laws favoring homosexuals have been used to assault religious freedom here.

The Train Has Left the Station

A Methodist retreat center in New Jersey lost a tax exemption in 2007[152] after it refused to let two lesbian couples use its facilities for their civil union ceremony. The Ocean Grove Camp Meeting Association, in existence since 1869, said it could not allow the same-sex ceremony because it believes that marriage is between a man and a woman, as does its parent denomination, the United Methodist Church. That religiously based objection is of no consequence in New Jersey, where same-sex civil unions became legal in 2007, and the state anti-discrimination law gives homosexuals special protected status.

"Our law against discrimination does not allow [the group] to use those personal preferences, no matter how deeply held, and no matter—even if they're religiously based—as a grounds to discriminate," an attorney for the lesbians told National Public Radio. "Religion shouldn't be about violating the law."[153]

New Mexico's human rights commission found the owners of a photography firm guilty of discrimination and fined them $6,600 in 2008 after its owners declined, based on Christian convictions, to photograph a commitment ceremony between two women. The owners are appealing the ruling, with assistance from the Alliance Defense Fund.[154]

Town clerks in Vermont have no choice under state law but to issue civil union certificates to homosexual couples, even if they object on religious grounds. Several clerks challenged that law, but lost their lawsuit to have that requirement removed.[155]

An Era of Intolerance

If town clerks can be required to violate their consciences, will ministers be forced to officiate for homosexual civil unions or "weddings?" "It is but a small step," according to the Liberty

"Gay-marriage proponents use the language of openness, tolerance and diversity, **... one foreseeable effect of their success will be to usher in an era of intolerance and discrimination the likes of which we have rarely seen before."**

—Mary Ann Glendon

Institute, "from requiring the issuance of civil union licenses to requiring the performing of solemnization ceremonies by ministers."[156]

Mary Ann Glendon, Learned Hand Professor of Law at Harvard University, warns that while "Gay-marriage proponents use the language of openness, tolerance and diversity, ... one foreseeable effect of their success will be to usher in an era of intolerance and discrimination the likes of which we have rarely seen before."[157]

Hate crime laws only escalate the conflict between religious liberty and homosexual rights. Anti-discrimination infractions can bring fines or a loss of tax-exemption; hate crime violations can mean time in prison. That is a possibility for pastors, since federal hate crime legislation would open the door for conspiracy convictions. A minister who preaches a message urging his congregation to oppose the homosexual agenda could be indicted for conspiracy to commit a crime, if one of his listeners acts in a way that is considered a violation of a federal hate crimes law.

Blaming Christians

"It is not difficult to imagine a situation in which a prosecutor might seek to link what they deem to be hateful speech to causing violent acts," said Rep. Lamar Smith (TX). "A chilling effect on religious leaders and others who express their constitutionally protected beliefs unfortunately could result."[158]

Attempts to link Christian speech to anti-homosexual violence have begun. The San Francisco Board of Supervisors lashed out at Christian groups after the murder of Matthew Shepard in 1998. The Board railed against an ad campaign featuring ex-homosexuals who found freedom through Christ and issued a proclamation charging that "An unfortunate, extreme result of these anti-gay campaigns is violence and even death."[159]

The executive director of the National Gay and Lesbian Task Force charged in 2005 that "The literal blood of thousands of gay people physically wounded by hatred during 2004 is on the hands of Jerry Falwell, James Dobson, Tony Perkins and so many others who spew hate for partisan gain and personal enrichment."[160]

Risk to Pastors

But would federal hate crimes legislation really open the door to conspiracy charges? Rep. Louis Gohmert (TX) pressed Rep. Artur Davis (AL) in 2007 during House Judiciary committee debate as to whether the amendment Davis offered would, in fact, shield ministers from conspiracy charges.

Gohmert: And if I understood the gentleman's amendment—and I will put the question back to you—if a minister preaches that sexual relations outside of marriage of a man and woman is wrong, and somebody within that congregation goes out and does an act of violence, and that person says that that minister counseled or induced him through the sermon to commit that act, are you saying under your amendment that in no way could that ever be introduced against the minister?

Mr. Davis: No.[161]

The purpose behind hate crime legislation is

"not to punish what is already illegal. It is to muzzle people of faith who dare to express their moral and biblical concerns about homosexuality."

—Dr. James Dobson

That terse but candid response from Rep. Davis, a graduate of Harvard Law School and a former federal prosecutor, highlights the potential risk pastors would face under a federal hate crime law.

Muzzling People of Faith

Even if indictments were not brought against pastors, the potential for prosecution will cause some ministers to keep silent. That may be the point, according to Dr. James Dobson, founder of Focus on the Family.

The purpose behind hate crime legislation, he said in 2007, is "not to punish what is already illegal. It is to muzzle people of faith who dare to express their moral and biblical concerns about homosexuality."[162]

Not only that, but hate crime legislation, if made the law of the land, would help convince courts to legalize same-sex "marriage."

TRUTH 10

Hate Crime Laws Advance the Homosexual Agenda

Advocates for homosexual rights made history in 1990 when they gathered around then President George H.W. Bush as he signed the Hate Crimes Statistics Act into law. The measure requires the Justice Department to count how many hate crimes are committed each year in America.

The ceremony at the Old Executive Office Building was historic on two fronts. First, the White House invited more than 20 homosexual activists to witness the event, something that had never been done. It was also, more significantly, "the first time in history that sexual orientation will be included in a federal civil rights law," as Tim McFeeley, executive director of the Human Rights Campaign, said.[163] The *Washington Blade*, a homosexual weekly, called it a "landmark development."[164] For President G. H. W. Bush, the event may have been meant to signal his "tolerance," but as one Washington observer put it, "what the bill is really all about is legitimacy for homosexuality."[165]

The Goal—Legitimacy

That is exactly what homosexual advocates had in mind in the mid-1980s when they enlisted Rep. Barney Frank, an open homosexual, to help add them to the list of victim groups in the proposed Hate Crimes Statistics Act. Inclusion for them was "an important first step toward official recognition of gay rights."[166]

For homosexuals, the long march to legitimacy—which includes same-sex marriage—is being taken one step at a time. They understand that legal recognition in one area of the law will pry open long-closed doors in others. That is why hate crime laws, which pose an immediate threat to free speech and religious liberty, also pose a long-term danger. They bring added legitimacy to the homosexual lifestyle and, on the federal level, enhance prospects that the U.S. Supreme Court will ultimately legalize same-sex marriage nationwide.

Law is incremental. Statutes such as hate crime laws can serve as stepping stones in a long-term strategy to remake criminal and family law. This strategy has been successful in the Netherlands, the first nation to legalize same-sex marriage, and in some states in the U.S.

Dispatching History

Laws granting recognition and special rights to homosexuals—including hate crime statutes—helped the Vermont, New Jersey, and California high courts to open the doors to civil unions or marriage for same-sex partners.

Vermont's Supreme Court struck down traditional marriage laws in 1999 by relying, in part, on earlier legislative actions. The high court first dispatched the weight of history by stating that "equal protection of the laws cannot be limited by eighteenth-century standards" and went on to say,

... whatever claim may be made in light of the undeniable fact that federal and state statutes—including those in Vermont—have historically disfavored same-sex relationships, more recent legislation plainly undermines the contention.[167]

The court noted that Vermont legislators:

- repealed a ban on oral sex in 1977;
- passed a hate crime law in 1989 that included "sexual orientation" as a protected category;
- prohibited discrimination based on "sexual orientation" in 1991;
- legalized adoption by same-sex couples;
- and gave certain rights to couples who end their "domestic relationship."

New Jersey's Supreme Court also relied on earlier laws favoring homosexuals in 2006 when it ruled that same-sex couples should be given the right to marry or to have civil unions. New Jersey first passed a hate crime law in 1981, and the state high court, in its ruling, cited the numerous ways in which New Jersey law already recognized homosexuals. The court determined,

FIRST STEPS: Laws giving homosexuals the right to civil unions and "marriage" rest on earlier grants of special rights to homosexuals, including hate crime laws.

(Douglas McFadd/ Boston Herald/Rapport Press)

> There is no rational basis for, on the one hand, giving gays and lesbians full civil rights in their status as individuals, and, on the other, giving them an incomplete set of rights when they follow the inclination of their sexual orientation and enter into committed same-sex relationships.[168]

California's Supreme Court also took notice of state laws barring discrimination based on "sexual orientation" when it gave homosexuals the right to marry in May 2008. The court said that the legislature had already granted same-sex couples "virtually all of the benefits and responsibilities afforded by California law to married opposite-sex couples"[169] According to the court,

> In light of the evolution of our state's understanding concerning the equal dignity and respect to which all persons are entitled without regard to their sexual orientation, it is not appropriate to interpret these provisions in a way that, as a practical matter, excludes gay individuals from the protective reach of such basic civil rights.[170]

An Incremental Approach

Homosexual rights advocates in California employed a succession of incremental legislative steps, including hate crime legislation (first made law in 1976[171]), to reach the long-sought goal of gaining the right to "marry." Dale Carpenter, a homosexual and a law school professor, wrote in 2004 that instead of "grabbing headlines with dramatic judicial victories," homosexuals in California "were quietly and patiently persuading state legislators to experiment with increasing degrees of legal protection for gay couples."[172]

The process, he said, has been so successful that "what started as almost nothing for gay partners in 1999 will have become shadow marriage by 2005."[173] All that remains is to overcome

the will of the people, who will vote again in November 2008 on whether marriage means a man and a woman.

The same step-by-step approach brought success in the Netherlands, the first nation to legalize homosexual marriage in 2001. Kees Waaldjik, the author of the Dutch same-sex marriage law, wrote that the path to marriage began with decriminalization of homosexual conduct, followed by anti-discrimination legislation, and then recognition of same-sex unions and parenting rights. Waaldjik wrote,

> ... once a legislature has enacted that it is wrong to treat someone differently because of his or her homosexual orientation, it becomes all the more suspect that the same legislature is preserving rules of family law that do precisely that.[174]

The High Court Opened the Door

The U.S. Supreme Court, which upheld a hate crime statute in 1994,[175] also advanced the cause of homosexual marriage by its 2003 decision striking down a Texas ban on sodomy. That ruling, *Lawrence v. Texas,* was relied on by the Massachusetts high court when it legalized same-sex marriage in late 2003.

Supreme Court Justice Antonin Scalia clearly expressed his view that the *Lawrence* decision would open the door to homosexual marriage, stating,

Today's opinion dismantles the structure of constitutional law that has permitted a distinction to be made between heterosexual and homosexual unions, insofar as formal recognition in marriage is concerned.[176]

Dr. D. James Kennedy

The late Dr. D. James Kennedy also warned that the *Lawrence* case would "place in the hands of homosexual activists a powerful tool to beat down resistance to their demands for the legalization of same-sex 'marriage.'"[177]

There can be little doubt that the cause of same-sex "marriage" will be strengthened and true marriage weakened if Congress acts to make proposed hate crime legislation law. The passage of a federal hate crime law granting special protection on the basis of "sexual orientation," would give homosexual activists one more argument to convince America's High Court that the time has come to legalize same-sex "marriage."

If that happens, the moral consequences to our nation will be devastating.

CONCLUSION

The State's Jurisdiction Is Over Citizen's Actions, Not Their Beliefs

At their root, hate crime laws violate the biblical model for civic government. The threat they pose to free speech, religious liberty, equal justice, and the family is a consequence of that violation.

The authors of hate crime laws claim for men a role reserved to God alone. They consign to civic rulers the right and authority to criminalize *thoughts and beliefs*. More preposterously, they presume that government is competent to identify the presence of prejudice and to discern whether any bias hidden inside a suspect's heart could have motivated a crime.

God Alone Is the Judge

None of that should be the prerogative of mere mortals. Government cannot adjudicate these "misty matters." God alone is judge of the heart of man. The black depths and inner mazes of our souls can be known only by our Maker, not by any human rights commission or federal prosecutor. As the Scripture states,

> The heart is deceitful above all things, And desperately wicked; Who can know it? I, the Lord, search the heart, I test the mind, Even to give every man according to his ways, According to the fruit of his doings (Jeremiah 17:9-10).

> For the Lord does not see as man sees; for man looks at the outward appearance, but the Lord looks at the heart" (I Samuel 16:7).
>
> For the word of God is living and powerful, and sharper than any two-edged sword, piercing even to the division of soul and spirit, and of joints and marrow, and is a discerner of the thoughts and intents of the heart. And there is no creature hidden from His sight, but all things are naked and open to the eyes of Him to whom we must give account (Hebrews 4:12-13).

The Limit of Civil Authority

Civil rulers have no business, according to the Bible, taking authority over what its citizens think. Jesus made it plain in the New Testament that civic rulers have limited authority. Asked whether it was lawful to pay taxes to Caesar, Jesus answered by declaring the separate jurisdictions of the state and God, "Render to Caesar the things that are Caesar's," he told his questioners, "and to God the things that are God's" (Mark 12:17).

The state's limited jurisdiction extends only to actions and not to beliefs, as the Apostle Paul made clear in his letter to the Romans. Note his choice of words as he describes the job function of civic rulers.

For he is God's minister to you for good. But if you *do evil*, be afraid; for he does not bear the sword in vain; for he is God's minister, an avenger to execute wrath on him who *practices evil* (Romans 13:4, emphasis added).

Paul warned his readers that they should be afraid if they *do evil*, not if they *think evil.* The state is an avenger on the one who *practices evil*, not the one who *thinks evil thoughts.*

But those who lobby and vote for hate crime laws pay no mind to the limits laid down by the Creator and, in so doing, they put all our liberties at risk.

"I had to learn to do something I had never done.
I had to get into God's Word and find out what it has to say about love."

—Johnny Lee Clary

God's Solution—Undeserved Grace

The way to eliminate hate is not through law, but grace. It is God's grace in Christ, not "enhanced sentencing" that will introduce love into hate-scarred hearts. That's what happened to Johnny Lee Clary, a former Grand Imperial Wizard of the White Knights of the Ku Klux Klan. Taught racism from the age of five, Clary spent 16 years with the Ku Klux Klan, rising to national prominence.

He later rejected Klan ideology and professed faith in Christ. He called a black pastor and civil rights leader to tell him about his change of heart. The pastor, Wade Watts, a former president of the Oklahoma NAACP, told Clary he had been praying for him

LEFT KLAN: Hate turned to love in Johnny Lee Clary's heart after he trusted Christ.

for years and invited the new believer to come speak at his church—a building Clary had once tried to burn down.

"I wouldn't tell you all the hate and prejudice left right then, because hatred is a learned response just like love is," Clary said of his commitment to Christ. "I had to learn to do something I had never done. I had to get into God's Word and find out what it has to say about love."[178]

There is a solution to hate—God's truth and His grace. Government can, and must, enforce long-standing laws prohibiting violent acts against people and property. It cannot—and should not—try to take God's place and rule over the hearts and minds of men and women. That role does not belong to civil governments; it is God's alone.

ENDNOTES

Introduction

1 *Hate Crimes Laws: Censoring the Church and Silencing Christians*, 2007 video from Family Research Council and Coral Ridge Ministries.

2 "War Launched on (Some) Crimes," *Impact* (newsletter of Coral Ridge Ministries), May 1999, p. 1.

3 *Hate Crimes Laws: Censoring the Church and Silencing Christians.*

4 "Anti-Defamation League State Hate Crime Statutory Provisions," Anti-Defamation League. http://www.adl.org/99hatecrime/state_hate_crime_laws.pdf

5 James B. Jacobs and Kimberly Potter, *Hate Crimes: Criminal Law & Identity Politics*, New York: Oxford University Press, 1998, p. 67.

6 Amy Worden and Angela Couloumbis, "Pa. hate-crime protections weakened," *Philadelphia Inquirer*, July 26, 2008. http://www.philly.com/inquirer/local/20080726_Pa__hate-crime_protections_weakened.html

7 James Madison, *Memorial and Remonstrance against Religious Assessments (1785).*

Truth 1: "Hate Crimes" Are Not Crimes of Hate

8 *West Virginia State Board Of Education v. Barnette*, 319 U.S. 624 (1943).

9 "New Details Emerge in Matthew Shepard Murder," ABC News, November 26, 2004. http://abcnews.go.com/2020/Story?id=277685&page=1

10 James Brooke, "Gay Man Dies From Attack, Fanning Outrage and Debate," *New York Times*, October 13, 1998, http://www.nytimes.com/ads/marketing/laramie/19981012_laramie3.html

11 "A Message Of Hope: Matthew Shepard Remembered At Vigils," CBS News, October 15, 1998. http://www.cbsnews.com/stories/1998/10/15/national/main20090.shtml

12 Richard Lacayo, "The New Gay Struggle," *Time*, October 26, 1998. http://www.time.com/time/magazine/article/0,9171,989406,00.html

13 "Mourners urge Congress to pass hate crime legislation," Associated Press, October 15, 1998.

14 "Gephardt Statement at Candlelight Vigil for Matthew Shepard," PR Newswire, October 15, 1998. http://www.encyclopedia.com/doc/1G1-53084201.html

15 Transcript of *Today Show*, Tuesday, October 13, 1998. Accessed at http://listserv.unl.edu/cgi-bin/wa?A2=ind9810&L=lmw-l&D=0&P=18432

16 "Court: City's Posture No Injury to Belief, Speech Rights," http://www.cfac.org/Stories/Stories_2002/free_speech_2002.html#anchor92130

17 "New Details Emerge," ABC News, November 26, 2004.

18 Bill Luckett, "TV show explores Shepard murder," *Caspar Star-Tribune*, November 24, 2004. http://www.trib.com/articles/2004/11/25/news/072dffe680abf84887256f56000fa206.txt

19 Luckett, "TV show explores."

20 "New Details Emerge," ABC News, November 26, 2004.

21 "New Details Emerge," ABC News, November 26, 2004.

22 Rochelle Riley, "Love left no room for hate at friend's wedding," *Detroit Free Press*, June 26, 2008.

23 Dave Cullen, "A dramatic moment of mercy: The Shepard family spares the life of their son's killer," November 5, 1999. http://www.salon.com/news/feature/1999/11/05/shepard/

Truth 2: Hate Crime Laws Are a Solution in Search of a Problem

24 Jack Levin, Jack McDevitt, *Hate Crimes: The Rising Tide of Bigotry and Bloodshed,* Boulder, CO: Westview Press, 2001, p. ix.

25 *A Policymaker's Guide to Hate Crimes*, Washington, D.C.: Bureau of Justice Assistance. U.S. Department of Justice, p. iii.

26 Opening Statement for Senator Benjamin L .Cardin, Confirmation Hearing, Senate Judiciary Committee December 18, 2007. http://judiciary.senate.gov/member_statement.cfm?id=3060&wit_id=6059.

27 Mark Potok, Luke Visconti, Barbara Frankel, and Nigel Holmes, "The Geography of Hate," *The New York Times*, November 25, 2007. http://www.nytimes.com/2007/11/25/opinion/25potok.html?scp=3&sq=hate+crimes&st=nyt

28 Hate Crime –1995, Uniform Crime Reports, Federal Bureau of Investigation. http://www.fbi.gov/ucr/hatecm.htm

29 "Incidents and Offenses," Hate Crime Statistics, 2006, Uniform Crime Report. http://www.fbi.gov/ucr/hc2006/downloadablepdfs/incidentsoffenses.pdf

30 Caroline Wolf Harlow, Ph.D., "Hate Crime Reported by Victims and Police," Bureau of Justice Statistics Special Report, November 2005, p. 2. http://www.ojp.usdoj.gov/bjs/pub/pdf/hcrvp.pdf

31 Harlow, p. 2.

32 "Hate Crime Data Collection Guidelines," Uniform Crime Reporting, Revised October 1999, Federal Bureau of Investigation, p. 23. http://www.fbi.gov/ucr/hatecrime.pdf

33 "Incidents and Offenses, 2006 Hate Crimes Statistics," Criminal Justice Information Services Division, Federal Bureau of Investigation, U.S. Department of Justice. http://www.fbi.gov/ucr/hc2006/incidents.html

34 "FBI Releases its 2006 Crime Statistics," September 24, 2007, Crimes in the United States, 2006, Uniform Crime Reports, Federal Bureau of Investigation. http://www.fbi.gov/ucr/cius2006/about/crime_summary.html

35 "Incidents and Offenses, 2006." U.S. Department of Justice.

36 The precise percentage is .0796399.

37 "Incidents and Offenses, 2006," U.S. Department of Justice.

38 The precise percentage is .0124108.

39 Carl Hulse, "Congressional Maneuvering Dooms Hate Crime Measure," *New York Times*, December 7, 2007. http://www.nytimes.com/2007/12/07/washington/07hate.html

40 Ala. Code § 13A-5-13 (1994). Cited in David Goldberger, "The Inherent Unfairness of Hate Crime Statutes," *Harvard Journal on Legislation*, Vol. 41, Num. 2, Summer 2004, p. 454. http://www.law.harvard.edu/students/orgs/jol/vol41_2/goldberger.php#fn36

41 Fla. Stat. Ann. §§ 775.085, 775.082 (West 2002). Cited in Goldberger, pp. 454-455.

42 Jack Levin, Jack McDevitt, *Hate Crimes: The Rising Tide of Bigotry and Bloodshed* , p. 100, emphasis in original. Quoted in James B. Jacobs and Kimberly Potter, *Hate Crimes: Criminal Law & Identity Politics*, New York: Oxford University Press, 1998, p. 81.

43 Phyllis B. Gerstenfeld, *Hate Crimes: Causes, Controls, and Controversies*, Thousand Oaks, CA: Sage Publications, 2004, p.235.

44 *Wisconsin v. Mitchell*, 113 S. Ct. at 2201. Quoted in Jacobs, Potter.

45 James B. Jacobs and Kimberly Potter, *Hate Crimes: Criminal Law & Identity Politics*, New York: Oxford University Press, 1998, p. 67.

46 Paul Iganski, "Hate Crimes Hurt More," in *Hate and Bias Crime: A Reader*, Barbara Perry, New York: Routledge, 2003, p. 135.

47 Jack Levin, Jack McDevitt, *Hate Crimes Revisited: America's War on Those Who Are Different*, Boulder, CO: Westview Press, 2002, p. 6.

48 "Incidents and Offenses, 2006," U.S. Department of Justice.

49 Daniel E. Troy, "Federal Hate Crimes Legislation," Testimony, House Judiciary Committee, August 4, 1999. http://www.aei.org/publications/pubID.17122,filter.all/pub_detail.as

Truth 3: Hate Crime Laws Criminalize Thought

50 *Hate Crimes Laws: Censoring the Church and Silencing Christians*, 2007 video by Coral Ridge Ministries and Family Research Council.

51 "Philadelphia Eleven File Suit In Federal Court Over 2004 'Outfest' Arrests," Repent America press release, October 13, 2005. http://www.repentamerica.com/pr_OutFest2004LegalChallenge.html

52 Ron Strom, "Christian group gets obscene, hateful messages," WorldNetDaily.com, January 18, 2005. http://www.worldnetdaily.com/news/article.asp?ARTICLE_ID=42417

53 *Hate Crimes Laws,"* 2007 video by Coral Ridge Ministries and Family Research Council.

54 Dr. D. James Kennedy interview with Dr. Frank Wright in *Hate Crimes Laws: Censoring the Church and Silencing Christians*, a video from Coral Ridge Ministries.

55 Thomas Jefferson, Letter to the Danbury Baptists, January 1, 1802. http://www.loc.gov/loc/lcib/9806/danpre.html

56 Gary Amos and Richard Gardiner, *Never Before in History: America's Inspired History* (Dallas, Texas: Haughton Publishing Company, 1998), 8.

57 Roger Williams, *The Bloody Tenet of Persecution*, 1644, in Page Smith, *Religious Origins of the American Revolution*, Missoula, MT: Scholar's Press, 1976, p. 122. Quoted in Gary Amos, Richard Gardiner, *Never Before in History: America's Inspired Birth,* Richards, Texas: Foundation for Thought and Ethics, 2004, p. 47.

58 The Westminster Confession of Faith (1646), chapter 20, para. 2. http://www.reformed.org/documents/index.html?mainframe=http://www.reformed.org/documents/westminster_conf_of_faith.html

59 The Virginia Act For Establishing Religious Freedom, 1786, http://religiousfreedom.lib.virginia.edu/sacred/vaact.html

60 Joseph Story, *Commentaries on the Constitution of the United States*, Vol. 2, Boston: Little, Brown, and Company, 1891, p. 631. Cited in Roy Moore, "What's not to love about 'hate crimes' laws?", WorldNetDaily.com, January 31, 2007. http://www.worldnetdaily.com/index.php?pageId=39939.

61 *United States v. Schwimmer*, 279 U.S. 644 (1929). http://supreme.justia.com/us/279/644/case.html

62 *Texas v. Johnson*, 491 U.S. 397 (1989). http://supreme.justia.com/us/491/397/index.html

63 Wendy Kaminer, "The Return of the Thought Police: 'Hate crime' legislation is an assault on civil liberties," *Wall Street Journal*, October 28, 2007. http://www.opinionjournal.com/editorial/feature.html?id=110010792

64 *State v. Wyant*, 597 N.E.2d 450 (1992), vacated and remanded, 113 S. Ct. 2954 (1993). Quoted in James B. Jacobs and Kimberly Potter, *Hate Crimes: Criminal Law & Identity Politics*, New York: Oxford University Press, 1998, p. 123.

65 Glen Lavy, "Hate Crime Report," Alliance Defense Fund, April 20, 2007, p. 6. http://www.telladf.org/UserDocs/HateCrimesReport.pdf

Truth 4: Hate Crime Laws Violate Equal Justice Under the Law

66 James B. Jacobs and Kimberly Potter, *Hate Crimes: Criminal Law & Identity Politics*, New York: Oxford University Press, 1998, p. 67.

67 "Hate Crime Legislation: Unequal Treatment Under The Law," Traditional Values Coalition Special Report,

p. 4. http://www.traditionalvalues.org/pdf_files/HateCrimes.pdf
68 Daniel E. Troy, "Federal Hate Crimes Legislation," Testimony, House Judiciary Committee, August 4, 1999. http://www.aei.org/publications/pubID.17122,filter.all/pub_detail.as
69 Ibid.
70 Herbert W. Titus, "Biblical Principles of Law," Regent University syllabus, 1984, p. 168.
71 Titus, p. 168.
72 Titus, p. 179.
73 *Strauder v. West Virginia*, 100 U.S. 303 (1879). http://supreme.justia.com/us/100/303/case.html
74 Justice John Marshall Harlan, Dissent to *Plessy v. Ferguson*, 163 U.S. 537 (1896), http://caselaw.lp.findlaw.com/scripts/getcase.pl?court=US&vol=163&invol=537
75 George Orwell, *Animal Farm*, New York: New American Library, 1946, p. 133.

Truth 5: Hate Crime Laws Are About Recognition, Not Fighting Crime

76 "Local Law Enforcement Hate Crimes Prevention Act of 2007," Report 110-113, pp. 17-31. http://frwebgate.access.gpo.gov/cgi-bin/getdoc.cgi?dbname=110_cong_reports&docid=f:hr113.110.pdf
77 Carl Hulse, "Congressional Maneuvering Dooms Hate Crime Measure," *New York Times*, December 7, 2007. http://www.nytimes.com/2007/12/07/washington/07hate.html
78 James B. Jacobs and Kimberly Potter, *Hate Crimes: Criminal Law & Identity Politics*, New York: Oxford University Press, 1998, p. 67.
79 Jacobs, Potter, p. 79.
80 New Jersey Governor Jim Florio, August 1990. Quoted in Jacobs, Potter, p. 65.
81 Letter from New York State Governor Mario M. Cuomo to the New York State Legislature, August 16, 1991. Quoted in Jacobs, Potter, p. 29.
82 Text of remarks delivered by State Representative Dan Ponder, Jr. in support of Hate Crimes Legislation, March 16, 2000. http://www.jfklibrary.org/Education+and+Public+Programs/Profile+in+Courage+Award/Award+Recipients/Dan+Ponder/Text+of+Speech+in+Support+of+Hate+Crime+Legislation.htm
83 Andrew H. Malcolm, "New Efforts Developing Against the Hate Crime," *New York Times*, May 12, 1989. http://query.nytimes.com/gst/fullpage.html?res=950DE1DE1E3DF931A25756C0A96F948260
84 Jacobs, Potter, p. 73.
85 "Child Abuse in America," Childhelp. http://www.childhelp.org/resources/learning-center/statistics/child-abuse-statistics
86 Jacobs, Potter, p. 41.
87 Jacobs, Potter, p. 72.
88 "Overview: Task Force's long history of working to secure hate crimes protections for LGBT people," National Gay and Lesbian Task Force. http://www.thetaskforce.org/issues/hate_crimes_main_page/overview

Truth 6: Hate Crime Laws Burden the Justice System

89 "A mother's story — what happened to Sean," http://www.seanslastwish.com/
90 Greg Hambrick, "North Charleston murder highlights absence of state hate crime law," Charleston City Paper, March 19, 2008. http://www.charlestoncitypaper.com/gyrobase/Content?oid=oid%3A42318
91 "Victim being gay not motive in slaying, investigator says," *Greenville News*, Dec. 1, 2007.

92 "Sean Kennedy's killer gets 10 months in jail," http://www.hatecrimesbill.org/2008/06/sean-kennedys-k.html

93 That may be misdirected effort since the real legislative fix needed is a state sentencing standard for involuntary manslaughter greater than the five year maximum available to prosecutors in South Carolina. A grand jury rejected a murder charge against Moller because there was no evidence of malicious intent. Prosecutors, faced with the possibility of Moller being released, brought the alternate charge of involuntary manslaughter under which Moller was convicted. A judge sentenced Moller to three years in June 2008.

94 James B. Jacobs and Kimberly Potter, *Hate Crimes: Criminal Law & Identity Politics*, New York: Oxford University Press, 1998, p. 67.

95 John Leo, *Two Steps Ahead of the Thought Police*, New Brunswick, New Jersey: Transaction Publishers, 1998, p. 70.

96 "Hate Crime Data Collection Guidelines," Rev. October 1999, U.S. Department of Justice, p. 2.

97 Ibid., p. 6.

98 Jacobs, Potter, p. 96.

99 Jeremy Pawloski, "Lawyer Complains of 'Public Frenzy,'" *Albuquerque Journal*, March 19, 2005.

100 Guy Molinari, "Don't Label Every Crime a Bias Incident," *New York Times*, February 6, 1992. http://query.nytimes.com/gst/fullpage.html?res=9E0CEEDD1038F935A35751C0A964958260

101 "The Larger Crime," *New York Times*, January 17, 1992. http://query.nytimes.com/gst/fullpage.html?res=9E0CE2DC1231F934A25752C0A964958260

102 Vanessa Hua, "Hate crime trial nears end: White juvenile accused of attack on Asian American teens," *San Francisco Chronicle*, July 12, 2004. http://www.sfgate.com/cgi-bin/article.cgi?file=/chronicle/archive/2004/07/12/BAGGP7K20E1.DTL

103 Jacobs, Potter, p. 106-107.

104 Jack Langer, "The Sensitivity Police: Where's American Multiculturalism Heading?" Human Events.com, 07/16/2008. http://www.humanevents.com/article.php?id=27536

Truth 7: Hate Crime Laws Are a Vehicle for Identity Politics

105 Leo C. Rosten, Leonard Q. Ross, *The Education of H*Y*M*A*N K*A*P*L*A*N*, New York: Harcourt Trade, 1968, p. 85.

106 Roger Kimball, "Thoughts on July 4, America, and multiculturalism," Pajamas Media, July 4, 2008. http://pajamasmedia.com/rogerkimball/2008/07/04/thoughts-on-the-july-4-america-and-multiculturalism/

107 Alejandro Portes and Rubén G. Rumbaut, *Legacies: The Story of the Immigrant Second Generation*, Berkeley: University of California Press, 2001, p. 157-158. Quoted in *E Pluribus Unum, The Bradley Project on America's National Identity*, p. 35. www.bradleyproject.org.

108 *E Pluribus Unum, The Bradley Project on America's National Identity*, p. 35. www.bradleyproject.org.

109 *E Pluribus Unum*, p. 15.

110 Arthur M. Schlesinger, Jr., *The Disuniting of America: Reflections on a Multicultural Society*, New York: W.W. Norton & Company, Inc., 1998, p. 20.

111 Schlesinger, p. 22.

112 Morgan Reynolds, "Hate Crime Laws and the Reversion to Medieval Society," *Veritas*, Winter 2001, Texas Public Policy Foundation, p. 6.

113 Daniel Troy, "Federal Hate Crimes Legislation," Testimony, House Judiciary Committee, August 4, 1999.

http://www.aei.org/publications/pubID.17122,filter.all/pub_detail.asp

114 Daniel Troy.

115 Daniel Troy.

116 James B. Jacobs and Kimberly Potter, *Hate Crimes: Criminal Law & Identity Politics*, New York: Oxford University Press, 1998, p. 67.

117 Charles Sykes, *A Nation of Victims*, New York: St. Martin's Press, 1992, p. 118.

118 Daniel Troy.

119 Jacobs, Potter, p. 144.

120 J. Hector St. John de Crevecoeur, "Letters from an American Farmer," in *The Monthly Review; or Literary Journal*, July-December 1782, Vol. LXVII., p. 145.

121 Morgan Reynolds, p. 6.

122 *E Pluribus Unum, The Bradley Project on America's National Identity*, p. 15. www.bradleyproject.org.

Truth 8: Hate Crime Laws Jeopardize Freedom of Speech

123 "Freedom of Religion on Trial in Sweden," http://www.akegreen.org/.

124 "Swedish minister jailed for 'anti-gay' speech," Catholic World News, July 6, 2004. http://www.cwnews.com/news/viewstory.cfm?recnum=30655

125 Dale Hurd, "Swedish Pastor Sentenced for 'Hate Speech,'" CBN.com, September 10, 2004. http://www.cbn.com/cbnnews/cwn/091004sweden.aspx

126 Dale Hurd.

127 "Sweden — Criminalizing Religious Speech — Ake Green," http://www.becketfund.org/index.php/case/93.html

128 Ake Green, video at http://www.alliancedefensefund.org/issues/religiousfreedom/internationallaw.aspx?cid=4244

129 "Muslim Council Agrees to Drop Hate-Speech Suit Against Aussie Pastors After BF Wins Appeal," The Becket Fund for Religious Liberty, June 26, 2007. http://www.becketfund.org/index.php/article/676.html.

130 "Muslim Council Agrees"

131 RAC speech

132 "Muslim Council Agrees"

133 "Muslim Council Agrees"

134 Ahdar, R. and Leigh, I., Religious Freedom in the Liberal State, OUP, 2005. Quoted in *The 'homophobic hatred' offence, free speech and religious liberty: Clause 126 of the Criminal Justice and Immigration Bill*, Newcastle upon Tyne, England: January 2008, p. 11.

135 Ahdar, R., and Leigh, I., p. 12.

136 Street preacher convicted by magistrates for displaying a sign saying homosexuality is immoral," Christian Institute, http://www.christian.org.uk/rel_liberties/cases/harry_hammond.htm

137 Ecclesiastical Case Reports, *Hammond v DPP*, Ecclesiastical Law Society, http://www.ecclawsoc.org.uk/cases/case14.shtml

138 "Couple quizzed by police for complaining about 'gay rights,'" The Christian Institute. http://www.christian.org.uk/rel_liberties/cases/roberts.htm#1

139 David Sanderson, "Police tell Christian couple view on gays 'close to hate crime,'" *The Times*, December 23, 2005. http://www.timesonline.co.uk/tol/news/uk/article782242.ece

140 Bishop: Gays should see a doctor," BBC News, November 8, 2003.

http://news.bbc.co.uk/1/hi/england/merseyside/3253499.stm

141 "No charges for bishop in gay row," BBC News, November 9, 2003. http://news.bbc.co.uk/2/hi/uk_news/3255461.stm

142 "MP reported—to police over 'gay' comments," Christian Institute, June 9, 2008. http://www.christian.org.uk/news/20080609/mp-reported-to-police-over-gay-comments/

143 Ahdar, R., and Leigh, I., p. 11.

144 Canada Criminal Code, Criminal Code, Part VIII: Offences Against the Person and Reputation, Hate Propaganda, Sec. 319. http://laws.justice.gc.ca/en/showdoc/cs/C-46/bo-ga:l_VIII-gb:s_318//en#anchorbo-ga:l_VIII-gb:s_318

145 "The Letter that Started It All," http://canadianpastor.blogspot.com/

146 Darren E. Lund, Complainant, and Stephen Boissoin and The Concerned Christian Coalition, Respondents, Decision on Remedy, Human Rights and Citizenship Commission, May 30, 2008. Inc. http://www.albertahumanrights.ab.ca/Lund_Darren_Remedy053008.pdf

147 Sarah McGinnis, "Former pastor appeals human rights ruling," *Calgary Herald*, July 01, 2008. http://www.canada.com/calgaryherald/news/city/story.html?id=85c5adb1-b056-4095-b51e-4853f9c9ecb4

Truth 9: Hate Crime Laws Threaten Religious Liberty

148 Transcript, Markup of H.R. 1592, The "Local Law Enforcement Hate Crimes Prevention Act Of 2007," U.S. House of Representatives Judiciary Committee, April 25, 2007, p. 193. http://judiciary.house.gov/hearings/transcripts/transcript070425.pdf

149 Transcript, Markup of H.R. 1592, ,p. 194.

150 Alan Sears, "'Hate Crimes' Legislation: A License To Kill The First Amendment," Townhall.com, October 2, 2007. http://www.townhall.com/columnists/AlanSears/2007/10/02/hate_crimes_legislation_a_license_to_kill_the_first_amendment?page=2

151 Hamil R. Harris, "Conservative Black Pastors Fight Bill on Hate Crimes. At Issue Are Sermons Against Homosexuality," *Washington Post*, April 28, 2007, Page B09. http://www.washingtonpost.com/wp-dyn/content/article/2007/04/27/AR2007042701899.html

152 Jill P. Capuzzo, "Group Loses Tax Break Over Gay Union Issue," *New York Times*, September 18, 2007.

153 Barbara Bradley Hagerty, "Gay Rights, Religious Liberties: A Three-Act Story," National Public Radio, June 16, 2008. http://www.npr.org/templates/story/story.php?storyId=91486340

154 Barbara Bradley Hagerty.

155 "The Impact Of Hate Crimes Laws Upon Religious Organizations And Clergy," Liberty Institute, p. 17. http://www.lc.org/media/9980/attachments/hatecrimes.pdf

156 "The Impact Of Hate Crimes Laws," p. 17.

157 Mary Ann Glendon, "For Better or for Worse? The federal marriage amendment would strike a blow for freedom," *Wall Street Journal*, February 25, 2004. http://www.opinionjournal.com/editorial/feature.html?id=110004735

158 Transcript, Markup of H.R. 1592, The "Local Law Enforcement Hate Crimes Prevention Act Of 2007," U.S. House of Representatives Judiciary Committee, April 25, 2007, pp. 56-57. http://judiciary.house.gov/hearings/transcripts/transcript070425.pdf

159 "The Impact Of Hate Crimes Laws, p. 8.

160 "Task Force Calls Rise in Anti-Gay Crime a Product of America's Anti-Gay Industry," Statement from Matt Foreman, Executive Director, National Gay and Lesbian Task Force, April 26, 2005, http://www.thetaskforce.org/media/release.cfm?releaseID=815. Quoted in "The Impact Of Hate Crimes Laws Upon Religious Organizations And Clergy," Liberty Institute, p. 7. http://www.lc.org/media/9980/attachments/hatecrimes.pdf

161 Transcript, Markup of H.R. 1592, p. 206.

162 Wendy Cloyd, "Dr. Dobson Asks the Nation to Oppose Hate-Crimes Bill," CitizenLink.com, May 1, 2007. http://www.citizenlink.org/content/A000004525.cfm

Truth 10: Hate Crime Laws Advance the Homosexual Agenda.

163 James B. Jacobs and Kimberly Potter, *Hate Crimes: Criminal Law & Identity Politics*, New York: Oxford University Press, 1998, p. 67.

164 William McGurn, "Mr. Bush's cautious embrace? - George Bush and gay rights movement," *National Review*, May 28, 1990. http://findarticles.com/p/articles/mi_m1282/is_n10_v42/ai_9051351

165 William McGurn, *National Review*, May 28, 1990.

166 Fernandez, Joseph M. 1991. "Bringing Hate Crimes Into Focus," Harvard Civil Rights, Civil Liberties Law Rev. 26:261, p. 274. Cited in Jacobs and Potter, p. 69.

167 *Baker v. State* (98-032), p. 38. http://www.vermont-archives.org/govhistory/governance/Impeach/pdf/98-032_op.pdf

168 *Mark Lewis and Dennis Winslow, et al. v. Gwendolyn L. Harris*, etc., et al. (A-68-05), p. 49. http://fl1.findlaw.com/news.findlaw.com/cnn/docs/glrts/lewisharris102506opn.pdf

169 In re Marriage Cases 5/15/08, p. 45. http://www.courtinfo.ca.gov/opinions/documents/S147999.PDF

170 In re Marriage Cases 5/15/08, p. 69-70.

171 California Civil Code Sec. 51.7. *David Venegas et al., County of Los Angeles et al.*, Concurring Opinion by Baxter, J, p.3. http://bulk.resource.org/courts.gov/states/Cal/S113301.PDF

172 Dale Carpenter, "Spousal Rights by Increments: California Shows the Way," Independent Gay Forum. http://www.indegayforum.org/news/show/26682.html

173 Dale Carpenter, "Spousal Rights by Increments: California Shows the Way."

174 Kees Waaldijk, "The 'Law of Small Change': How the Road to Same-Sex Marriage Got Paved in the Netherlands," June 19, 1999, Paper for: Legal Recognition of Same-Sex partnerships: a Conference on National, European, and International Law, King's College, University of London, 1 to 3 July 1999. Quoted in "The Impact Of Hate Crimes Laws Upon Religious Organizations And Clergy," Liberty Counsel, p. 12.

175 *Wisconsin v. Mitchell*, (92-515), 508 U.S. 47 (1993).

176 *Lawrence v. Texas* (02-102) 539 U.S. 558 (2003), pp. 20-21. http://www.law.cornell.edu/supct/pdf/02-102P.ZD

177 "D. James Kennedy labels Lawrence Ruling a 'Declaration of Secular Supremacy,'" Press release from Coral Ridge Ministries, June 26, 2003.

Conclusion: The State's Jurisdiction is Over Citizens Actions, Not Their Beliefs

178 Dana Williamson, "Not a chance encounter, but a divine appointment with truth," Baptist Press, February 7, 2003. http://www.sbcbaptistpress.org/bpnews.asp?id=15196

TAKE THE NEXT STEP!

Video, Website to Help You Learn More!

Once you've read *Ten Truths About Hate Crime Laws*, ask for the video, *The Assault on Liberty*, featuring leaders and experts Robert Knight, Tristan Emmanuel, Matt Barber, and Dawn Stefanowicz. This in-depth DVD offers a lively and well-informed discussion moderated by Coral Ridge Ministries host Jerry Newcombe on how hate crime laws attack free speech and religious liberty in the U.S., Canada, and elsewhere. To request *The Assault on Liberty*, please call 1-800-988-7884 or go to www.coralridge.org.

Free Resources for Small Group Study!

Plus, please visit the Ten Truths About Hate Crime Laws section on our website at www.coralridge.org. Just click on the "Equip and Grow" tab and you'll find more resources for personal or small group study, including the online text of this booklet, a downloadable PowerPoint presentation, and a handy one-page Ten Truths About Hate Crime Laws Talking Points.

ABOUT THE AUTHOR

John Aman has been a writer/editor at Coral Ridge Ministries for 16 years. The author of *Ten Truths About Christians and Politics*, he is also a scriptwriter for *Learn2Discern*, the daily video news commentary from Coral Ridge Ministries. He has served as a writer for *Impact*, Coral Ridge Ministries' monthly newsletter, and has been general editor for more than 40 Coral Ridge Ministries-produced books or booklets. John has a masters degree in journalism and public policy from Regent University and has worked in Washington, D.C., as a news/talk radio program producer. He is active in the pro-life cause, serving as president of Broward County Right to Life. John and his wife, Tewannah, herself a pro-life leader and speaker, live in Fort Lauderdale, Florida.